Local Authority Companies 1996

1st Edition 1996

ISBN 0 904677 77 X
Published by LGC Communications,
33-39 Bowling Green Lane,
London EC1R 0DA.
Telephone: 0171 505 8555 Fax: 0171 278 8124

LGC Communications is part of EMAP Business Communications.

Printed by Nuffield Press.

Acknowledgement

Oyex forms H and I were reproduced by kind permission of The Solicitors' Law Stationery Society Limited for educational purposes only.

2

Contents

Introduction

The changing role of local authorities from 'providers' to 'enablers', the externalisation of core services, and the private finance initiative mean that senior managers are having to acquire a range of new commercial specialisations beyond traditional local government work. The formation and management of local authority companies is one aspect of this.

Companies may be set up: as part of a public/private sector joint venture project, as a co-ordinating body in the context of economic regeneration, to externalise an existing 'in house' function, or for community projects.

Local authority companies occupy a peculiar legal position in that they fall under the dual control of the Companies Act 1985 and its associated legislation, as well as public sector legal and financial constraints. A breach of either can leave directors and officers of a local authority company exposed to personal liability. The law relating to local authority companies is still in many respects uncertain – in particular as regards the powers of councils to set up companies.

Part V of the Local Government and Housing Act 1989 does not give councils any new powers to set up companies, nor does it even clarify the existing law in this respect. However, it laid the foundations for future regulation of council companies.

Six years later, the Local Authorities (Companies) Order 1995 provided a regulatory regime for companies which a local authority either controls or dominates.

This book examines both legal and practical issues involving local authority companies, ie: powers to set up; regulation under the 1995 Order; choices of company structure; company formation; duties and liabilities of company officers; protection from risk; and insurance. Basic precedents are included for illustration.

Complex statutory provisions have been summarised in the interest of readability, where this can be done without losing the original meaning. The following abbreviations are used throughout the text:

- LGHA – Local Government and Housing Act 1989

- LACO – Local Authorities (Companies) Order 1995 (as amended)

- CA – Companies Act 1985 (as amended).

Appendices H and I are reproduced by kind permission of the Solicitors' Law Stationery Society Ltd. for educational purposes only.

CHAPTER 1

Power to Form Companies

For some purposes Parliament has given councils specific powers to set up limited companies. But the extent to which councils can rely on their general powers to set up companies remains uncertain, although statute appears to allow this in appropriate circumstances.

A council which promotes, participates in or invests in a company without statutory authority is not only acting unlawfully, but may also be putting at risk the interests of any third party which deals with the company. Several financial institutions have already lost out badly when projects involving local authority companies have been ruled *ultra vires*.

Until recently the Audit Commission has maintained that a local authority may only establish or participate in a company where statute specifically provides. Recent High Court decisions may, however, force the Commission to change its thinking in this respect, if upheld by the appeal courts. The statutory provisions which either specifically or appear to give general powers to set up local authority companies can be summarised as follows.

Specific powers

Specific company formation powers – and duties – exist in respect of some public health and transport related utilities. Generally these require a local authority to establish a limited company to take over a relevant utility and its assets and liabilities in accordance with a scheme approved by the secretary of state. Such enabling legislation is normally self-contained as regards: the type of company to be formed, how it is to be managed, the purchase and sale of shares and other assets, the relationship between the company and its controlling authority, and how its functions are to be carried out.

Examples of such legislation are:
- section 67 Transport Act 1985 – formation of a company with share capital to take over a council's bus undertaking

7

- section 13 Airports Act 1986 – transfer of municipal airports to companies owned by local authorities.
- section 32 and Part I Schedule 2 Environmental Protection Act 1990 – requirement for waste disposal authorities to form or participate in the formation of waste disposal authorities and transfer the relevant part of their undertakings to it. The company must in each case be: limited by share capital, a wholly owned subsidiary of the relevant participating authorities, and an 'arm's length' company for the purposes of the Part V LGHA.

A local authority may promote, assist and guarantee the debts of a housing association using powers contained in section 58 Housing Act 1985. This may include the making of grants or loans, or the acquisition of share or loan capital in the association.

With some exceptions, financial assistance and guarantees may only be given for a housing association which is registered with the Housing Corporation – or Scottish Homes or Housing for Wales. To qualify for registration under section 3 of the 1985 Act, the association must be either a registered charity or an industrial and provident society (I & P) registered under the Industrial and Provident Societies Act 1965. It must be non-profit making and have among its objectives, the provision, construction, improvement or management of: houses for letting, hostels or houses where occupation is restricted to members of the association.

Within these constraints councils may choose the appropriate corporate structure (usually a company limited by guarantee or an I & P) if indeed it is necessary to incorporate at all. Section 1 of the 1985 Act envisages that a housing association may exist simply as an unincorporated society or body of trustees.

General powers

Section 33 LGHA 1989 allows councils to take such steps as are appropriate to promote economic development in their areas. This may include the setting up or expansion of any commercial, industrial or public undertaking where this will create local employment. Councils may also provide financial assistance including grants, loans, indemnities, acquire share or loan capital, or provide benefits in kind.

Sections 34 and 35 restrict and govern the manner in which assistance can be provided. Councils must have regard to government guidance and pre-programme assistance for the following year in consultation with individuals and organisations representing local commerce and industry.

The Local Government (Promotion of Economic Development) Regulations

1990 (as amended) further restrict the type of assistance which councils can provide under section 33. Thus, councils cannot, under section 33:

- provide general financial estate agency services; company audits; commercial valuations; acquire goods and services to resell, hire out, or supply to others; or employ people to manufacture goods
- grant an interest in land (other than by way of a short tenancy) at less than full market value in accordance with section 123 Local Government Act 1972
- provide financial assistance by way of a grant, loan or guarantee to a person conducting a business with a view to profit if the amount of such assistance is determinable by reference to the future financial results of that business, or if it is to be used to pay wages or salaries, unless (in either case) it is in the form of a grant which will:
  i) provide employment for someone who was previously unemployed
  ii) employ a person during training, or
  iii) employ not more than three persons with special knowledge or skill
- a council which is not an education authority may not provide education (other than to members or staff of that authority) except in consultation with the local education authority
- acquire land outside its area, or provide financial assistance to another person for the acquisition or improvement of such land, or the provision of plant and machinery – other than in consultation with the relevant local authority for the area within which the land is situated
- provide a loan at less than the market rate of interest unless the accounts of the authority reveal the exact amount of the hidden subsidy.

Section 145 Local Government Act 1972 allows a county or district council to do anything (whether inside or outside its area) which is necessary or expedient for:
a) provision of entertainment, dancing, theatres, concert or dance halls or similar facilities
b) maintenance of a band or orchestra
c) development and improvement of the knowledge, understanding and promotion of the arts and artistic crafts
d) incidental purposes including provision of refreshments, programmes and publicity.

When used in conjunction with section 111 Local Government Act 1972 *(see below)* the wide section 145 powers conceivably include the setting up of theatres and other companies.

Headed 'subsidiary powers', section 111 Local Government Act 1972 gives a local authority a general power to do anything (whether or not involving the expenditure, borrowing or lending of money or the acquisition or disposal of any property or rights) which is calculated to facilitate or is conducive or incidental to the discharge of its functions. The scope of section 111 is limited by two factors:

- section 111 is not a 'stand alone' power. It can only be used in conjunction with other statutory powers (eg. section 145 LGA 1972 or section 33 LGHA 1989) for an objective which is within the powers of the local authority
- section 111 takes subject to the provisions of any other enactment. This was illustrated in *Morgan Grenfell v London Borough of Sutton, Times, 23 March 1995.*

To enable Wellesley Housing Association to purchase housing to accommodate homeless families, Sutton LBC guaranteed loans made to it by Morgan Grenfell. However, Justice Clarke held the arrangement to be *ultra vires* because section 60 Housing Associations Act 1985 only allows councils to guarantee the liabilities of registered housing associations – which Wellesley was not. Section 111 could not over-ride this limitation. Morgan's £790,929.20 claim against the council failed.

In *Hazell v Hammersmith and Fulham LBC 89 LGR paragraph 271*, the House of Lords ruled that section 111 did not authorise interest rate 'swap' transactions *inter alia* because Part I Schedule 13 Local Government Act 1972 had established a comprehensive code which defined and limited the powers of a local authority with regard to borrowing.

In relation to the setting up of local authority companies, the scope of section 111 has been considered in two High Court cases.

Credit Suisse v Allerdale BC (first instance judgement 6 May 1994) concerned a joint venture to redevelop the old Keswick railway station site to create a leisure complex to include swimming pool, theatre, conference centre, squash and tennis courts. The cost of providing these facilities would be cross-subsidised by the simultaneous development and sale of time-share accommodation. But £6 million would first have to be raised to kick-start the development.

The council could not provide this money directly without going outside its statutory spending and borrowing constraints. Instead the council set up its own limited company, Allerdale Development Company, and guaranteed its borrowings. On this basis Credit Suisse agreed to fund the development.

Before entering into the arrangement, Allerdale took senior counsel's advice and wrote to the district auditor setting out its proposal. A financial projection showed that profits from time-share sales would pay for the leisure complex, with cash to spare. No one foresaw the 1988/89 property market collapse.

Only 175 time-share weeks were sold out of 1,000. The company could not repay the first instalment on its loan. The district auditor then wrote saying that in his provisional view the establishment of a company and the giving of a loan guarantee was outside the council's powers. Credit Suisse sued the council.

Rejecting the claim at first instance, Justice Coleman saw no reason in principle why a council could not set up a company under section 111 saying *inter alia*:

"When a local authority sets up a company as a means of carrying out a statutory function, it does not necessarily follow that the functions of the company will be other than those which the local authority itself could carry out or that the company will in practice be able to perform functions not lawfully open to the local authority, having regard in particular to the measure of control over the activities of that company which, the local authority retains by its ability to control decisions of the board of directors.

"Nor does it necessarily follow that the local authority will delegate to the company any of its decision making functions. Thus, it quite possible to envisage a company set up only for the purpose of carrying out a particular function and to which a local authority had delegated no more than ministerial or day-to-day decision-making of the kind which could in any event have been delegated by it to an independent contractor".

As regards the loan-guarantee he added *inter alia*:

"In my judgement, the guarantee by a local authority of the obligation of a company set up by the local authority to provide recreational facilities under section 19 [Local Government Miscellaneous Provisions Act 1976] is not necessarily impermissible any more than is the setting up of the company itself.

"...in order to decide in any given case whether a guarantee is within the local authority's incidental powers, it is necessary to ask what is the nature and purpose of the obligation performance of which is guaranteed".

But Justice Coleman held Allerdale's arrangement to be unlawful for two reasons:
- the purpose of the company was to avoid normal spending and borrowing constraints, therefore it had to be *ultra vires*
- the project itself was *ultra vires* as it is no part of a council's function to develop and sell time-share accommodation.

On appeal *(Times, 20 May 1996)*, the Court of Appeal unanimously upheld Justice Coleman's decision that the company and the loan guarantee were *ultra vires*. Delivering judgment, Neill LJ said, *inter alia*:

11

"The implied powers in section 111 did not provide an escape route from the statutory controls. That was clear not only as a matter of principle but also on the construction of section 111 itself. Section 111(3) ensured that the powers exercisable under section 111 had to be used in conformity with the other statutory provisions.

"Accordingly, the Bank's argument on statutory powers failed at each stage. The establishment of the company and the giving of the guarantee were part of an ingenious scheme designed to circumvent the no doubt irksome controls imposed by central government. The council however could only do what it was empowered to do by statute. Neither the establishment of a company nor the giving of a guarantee fell within its express or implied powers. In the light of that conclusion it followed that the establishment of the company and the giving of the guarantee were *ultra vires* acts".

In a decision given the same day *(Times, 20 May 1996)*, and for similar reasons, the Court of Appeal reversed Justice Gatehouse's earlier decision in *Credit Suisse v Waltham Forest LBC (Times, 2 November 1994)*, when he had upheld both the formation of a company and the giving of a loan guarantee.

Waltham Forest LBC did not have sufficient accommodation to fulfil its duties towards homeless people and was putting families into bed and breakfast accommodation.

To overcome this problem the council formed a joint venture company with a private sector partner which specialised in housing finance and leasing. The new company would buy houses on mortgage and lease them to the council on short-term tenancies. Waltham Forest would pay a full market rent for each of the properties, for which it would qualify for a housing subsidy. The company would in turn use its rental income to service the loan. At the end of the lease-period the houses would be sold and the proceeds used to pay off the loan.

On this basis Credit Suisse loaned £9m to the new company. Unfortunately tumbling property prices meant that when the properties were eventually sold, the proceeds were insufficient to clear the debt. Credit Suisse applied for summary judgement against the council and won.

Justice Gatehouse said at first instance that the council had a duty to accommodate homeless people, and power to buy houses for this purpose. In this case the council had acquired the house by leasing them from the company, which it could not have done without giving a loan guarantee. Therefore, the giving of the guarantee was conducive to the discharge of the council's homeless duties and was within section 111. The Court of Appeal disagreed and ruled that the arrangement was *ultra vires*.

Neill LJ said, *inter alia:*

"Section 101 (Local Government Act 1972) contained provisions relating to what arrangements could be made for the discharge of functions by local authorities. These powers were very limited and did not entitle a local housing authority to discharge any of their functions by means of a partly owned company.

"Could that power, or the power to give such a company assistance in the form of a guarantee or indemnity be implied by reason of section 111?"

He calculated that where parliament had made detailed provisions as to how certain statutory functions were to be carried out, there was no scope for implying the existence of additional powers which are wholly outside the statutory code.

CHAPTER 2

Statutory Provisions Relating to Local Authority Companies

Part V Local Government and Housing Act 1989 (LGHA) as supplemented by the Local Authorities (Companies) Order (SI 1995/849) as amended by SI 1996/621 (LACO) provides the statutory framework governing companies which local authorities control, influence or have a minority interest in. But note:

- that these controls, which affect only local authority companies, are in addition to the provisions of the Companies Act 1985 (as amended) (CA) and subsidiary legislation which affects all limited companies
- neither Part V nor the 1995 regulations give local authorities any new powers to set up or participate in the formation of limited companies. They only regulate the situation when such powers already exist to form companies *(see Chapter 1)*
- companies can drift in and out of LACO regulation from time to time depending on membership of the company and other circumstances.

Part V LGHA was passed at a time of mounting government concern that some councils were using companies to avoid controls on capital spending and borrowing which would otherwise apply. There were also doubts about the legal ability of councils to form and participate in limited companies. Six years later, when the regulations were made, government attitudes had changed. Local authority companies are now recognised as an appropriate vehicle to undertake a range of functions and objectives as part of the government's private finance initiative.

Part V Local Government and Housing Act 1989

Sections 67 to 73 LGHA provided the statutory framework for future regulation of local authority companies (which are deemed to include industrial and provident societies). For legislative convenience, Part V categorises local authority companies as: controlled, influenced, arm's length or minority interest companies. Each of these categories is considered below.

Council controlled companies

Section 68 LGHA deems a company to be under the control of a local authority in any of the following circumstances:
i) the company is a subsidiary of the local authority for the purposes of section 736 CA. Section 736 defines a company as being a subsidiary of a holding company if the holding company:
   a) holds a majority of voting rights in the subsidiary, or
   b) is a member of the subsidiary and has the right to appoint or remove a majority of the board of directors, or
   c) is a member of the subsidiary and controls alone, pursuant to an agreement with other shareholders or members, a majority of the voting rights in it.
ii) section 736 does not apply but the local authority has power to appoint or remove a majority of the board of directors of the company; or
iii) the company is under the control of another company which is itself under local authority control.

For the purposes of section 736, a company is a 'wholly owned subsidiary' if it has no members other than the holding company or another subsidiary of the holding company.

Section 68 (3) LGHA states that the power of a local authority to control the majority of votes at a general meeting of the company is reference to a power which is exercisable:
a) in the case of a company limited by shares: through the holding of equity share capital by the local authority, by nominees of the local authority or by persons whose shareholding is under the control of the local authority
b) in the case of any company through the holding of votes at a general meeting of the company by the local authority, by a group of members of the company the composition of which is controlled by the local authority, or by persons who have contractually bound themselves to vote in accordance with instructions of the local authority.

Section 68 (5) deems a person's shareholding to be under the control of a local authority if:
a) their right to hold the shares arose because of some action which the authority took, or refrained from taking, to enable them to have the right
b) the local authority, alone or jointly with one or more other persons, can require them to transfer their share holding (or part of it) to another person.

Arm's length companies

Section 68 (6) LGHA defines a local authority controlled company to be an 'arm's length' company for any financial year if:

a) before the beginning of that financial year the local authority passed a resolution that the company should be 'arm's length'
b) since the passing of that resolution and up to the end of the financial year in question, the following conditions have been satisfied while the company has been under local authority control:
i) each director has been appointed for a fixed term of at least two years
ii) unless the secretary of state otherwise directs under section 68 (7) LGHA, no director has been removed by resolution under section 303 CA.

Section 303 CA gives company members a statutory right to pass an ordinary resolution to remove a director before the expiration of their period of office, notwithstanding anything in the company's articles or any agreement between them and the company. But any right to damages or compensation consequent on termination of the director's appointment is preserved. Section 68 (7) LGHA allows the secretary of state to disregard the removal of a director under section 303 CA so long as he was not removed with a view to influencing the management of the company for non-commercial reasons.

Local authority influenced companies

Section 69 (1) LGHA defines a company to be under the influence of a local authority if the following conditions are met:
a) it is not a controlled company as defined by section 68
b) it is not a banking or insurance company or a member of a banking or insurance group
c) at least 20% of total voting rights are held by persons associated with the local authority or at least 20% of directors are so associated, or at least 20% of the total voting rights at a director's meeting are held by associated persons – and
d) there is a 'business relationship' between the company and the local authority as defined by section 69 (3) LGHA.

The term 'associated with a local authority' is widely defined by section 69 (5) LGHA to include: anyone who is a member or officer of the local authority; an employee who is also a director, manager, secretary or other similar officer of another company under the control of the authority; or someone who has been a councillor of the authority within the preceding four years.

It would also seem from the wording of section 69 (5) that a councillor or officer is deemed to be 'associated' even if his membership of the company is in some other non-local authority capacity, eg. as representing a voluntary group.

In addition, section 69 (6) LGHA states that the secretary of state may by order extend the definition of 'associated person' so that a person is at any time associated with a local authority if:

16

a) at that time they are, or are employed by, a subsidiary of a person who for the time being has a contractual relationship with the authority to provide:
i) advice with regard to the authority's interest in any company (whether existing or proposed)
ii) advice with regards to the management of an undertaking or the development of land by a company (whether existing or proposed to be formed) with which it is proposed that the authority should enter into any lease, license or other contract or to which it is proposed that the authority should make a grant or loan
iii) services which facilitate the exercise of the authority's rights in any company (whether by acting as the authority's representative at a meeting of the company or as a director appointed by the authority or otherwise)
b) at any time within the preceding four years they have been associated with the authority by virtue of subsection 69 (5)
c) they are at the time married to, or a business partner of, a person associated with the authority by virtue of subsection 69 (5) (a)
d) they hold a relevant office in a political association or other body which in the nomination paper of a person who is an elected member of the authority, formed part of that person's description.

A 'business relationship' between the company and the local authority as defined by section 69 (3) LGHA, will arise in any of the following circumstances if:
a) within a 12 month period the aggregate of payments to the company by the authority or by another company which is under the control of the authority represents more than one half of the company's turnover, as shown in its profit and loss account
b) more than one half of the company's turnover is derived from the exploitation of assets of any description in which the local authority or a company under the control of the authority has an interest (disregarding an interest in land which is in reversion on a lease granted for more than seven years)
c) the aggregate of:
i) grants made either by the authority and being expenditure for capital purposes or by a company under the control of the authority, and
ii) the nominal value of shares or stock in the company which is owned by the authority or by a company under the control of the authority, exceeds one half of the net assets of the company
d) the aggregate of:
i) grants falling within paragraph (c) (i) above,
ii) loans or other advances made or guaranteed by the authority or by a company under the control of the local authority, and
iii) the nominal value referred to in paragraph (c) (2) above, exceeds one half of the fixed and current assets of the company
e) the company at any time occupies land by virtue of an interest which it obtained from the local authority or a company under the control of the

local authority and which it so obtained at less than the best consideration reasonably obtainable

f) the company intends at that time to enter into (or complete) a transaction and, when that is done, there will then be a business relationship between the company and the authority by virtue of paragraphs (a) to (e) above.

The term 'net assets' is construed in accordance with section 152 (2) CA and means the aggregate of the company's assets less the aggregate of its liabilities (including amounts retained or reasonably necessary to provide for any liability or loss which is either likely to be incurred or certain to be incurred but uncertain as to the amount or as to the date at which it will arise).

Exemptions

Sections 68 (1) and 69 (1) LGHA allow the secretary of state to direct that a particular company or companies which would otherwise be controlled or influenced for the purposes of Part V LGHA are deemed not be so controlled or influenced. Such directions may be limited in time and subject to appropriate conditions.

The government has published a statement of its current intentions on exemptions. These are:

1. The following companies which would otherwise be controlled companies for the purposes of section 68, will not be so:

    i) Groundwork Trusts in England and Wales receiving central government funding grants;

    ii) Area Museum Councils in England and the Council of Museums in Wales;

    iii) Regional and Area Arts Boards in England and Regional Area Arts Associations in Wales;

    iv) National Housing and Town Planning Council (NHTPC);

    v) Building preservation trusts which are registered with the Architectural Heritage Foundation Fund and are under the control of one or more local authorities.

2. The following companies, which would otherwise be influenced companies, will not be so:

    i) a company financed by a revenue support grant under section 78 (1) Local Government Finance Act 1988

    (This effectively exempts the following bodies: Local Government Management Board; Fire Services Examination Boards; National Foundation for Education Research; the Staff College; National Institute of Adult Continuing Education; Local Government International Bureau; Local Authorities Co-ordinating Body on Food and Trading Standards; Commission for Local Administration in England).

    ii) a company where the only financial link with the local authority is a donation of £2,000 or less in any year

iii) a company which is a member of the National Association of Citizen's Advice Bureaux

iv) a housing association registered with the Housing Corporation.

v) a building preservation trust which is registered with the Architectural Heritage Fund

vi) a regional trust board in England.

The government will consider favourably applications for directions to exempt influenced companies which meet the following criteria:

a) the company is set up solely for registered charitable purposes

b) fewer than half of the directors are associated with one local authority

c) the company is managed independently of the local authority

d) in settling the terms of any transaction with the company the local authority has not undertaken to guarantee or indemnify (including by way of grant) the company against any future liability or loss.

The government has said that it will consider carefully on a case by case basis any other applications for directions under sections 68 (1) and 69 (1) LGHA.

Minority interest companies

Section 71 LGHA applies to companies other than controlled or influenced companies in which a local authority has an interest and which are for convenience referred to as 'minority interest companies'.

Section 71 (2) LGHA prohibits a local authority from buying shares, becoming a member, nominating members, appointing directors, or permitting a council officer to make any nomination or appointment or themselves become or remain a member or director of a minority interest company, unless that company is an 'authorised company' for the purposes of section 71 (1)(b).

This is not as restrictive as it first appears as Article 11 LACO defines as 'authorised' any company (other than a company regulated under that Order) in which a person associated with a local authority has a right to vote at a general meeting or of which any such person is a director.

Regulated and unregulated companies

Section 70 LGHA allows the secretary of state to make regulations relating to companies which are local authority controlled or influenced. It is the duty of a local authority to comply with such regulations in relation to any company under its control or influence. The sanction for non-compliance is that any payment made to the company, or otherwise incurred, contrary to regulations is deemed to be unlawful expenditure for the purposes of Part III Local Government Finance Act 1982 (accounts and audits). Thus, any person responsible for incurring or authorising such unauthorised expenditure can be ordered to repay it and (in the case of a councillor) may be disqualified from membership of the local authority.

It is pursuant to section 70 that LACO was made. Its main provisions came into effect on 1 April 1995, although regulated companies had until 1 July 1995 to comply with regulation 4 relating to company notepaper and other company documents.

Under LACO the main distinction is not between controlled, influenced or minority interest companies, but between 'public sector led' companies which are regulated and 'private sector led' companies which are not.

Article 1 (4) LACO defines a local authority company to be 'regulated' if:
a) it is a 'controlled company' for the purposes of section 68 LGHA; or
b) it is an 'influenced company' for the purposes of section 69 and it is either an unlimited company or an industrial and provident society, or it is an influenced company and satisfies one of the following two tests:
Test 1: the authority would, if it were itself a limited company, be treated by section 258 CA as having the right to exercise a 'dominant influence' over the company in question
Test 2: if the authority were a company registered under the CA it would be required under section 227, or applicable accounting standards, to prepare group accounts for the company in question.

The phrase 'dominant influence' for the purpose of Test 1 is poorly defined. Paragraph 4 (1) schedule 10 (A) CA states simply that for the purposes of section 258 (2) an undertaking shall not be regarded as having the right to exercise a dominant influence over another undertaking unless it has the right to give directions with respect to operating and financial policies of the other undertaking to which its directors are obliged to comply whether or not they are for the benefit of that undertaking.

Financial Reporting Standard 2 (FRS2), published by the Accounting Standards Board, states that the actual exercise of dominant influence is:

"The exercise of an influence that achieves the result that the operating and financial policies of the undertaking influenced are set in accordance with the wishes of the holder of the influence and for the holder's benefit, whether or not those wishes are explicit. The actual exercise of dominant influence is identified by its effect in practice rather than by the way in which it is exercised".

Section 258 (2) CA states that an undertaking is a parent undertaking in relation to a subsidiary if, *inter alia*:

"Section 258 (2) (c), it has the right to exercise a dominant influence over the undertaking by virtue of:
1. the undertaking's memorandum and articles or
2. a control contract (ie. a contract conferring a right which is authorised by the memorandum and articles and which is permitted by the law under which that undertaking was formed)".

For the purpose of Test 2, section 227 CA states that at the end of a financial year, the directors of a parent company must, as well as preparing individual accounts for the company, prepare group accounts.

It will be seen that whilst local authority control or influence is a pre-condition of regulation under LACO, an influenced company limited by shares will only be regulated if it passes either Test 1 or Test 2 above, or both. Influenced share capital companies which pass neither of these tests will be in the same position as any other unregulated minority interest company.

Other companies expressly excluded from LACO are:
- a public transport company within section 72 Transport Act 1985
- a public airport company within Part II Airports Act 1986
- a company under the control or influence of a Passenger Transport Executive
- a company which by virtue of section 73 LGHA is treated as under the control or subject to the influence of two or more authorities, where each of those authorities is a Passenger Transport Executive
- a company which in relation to a company ('the holding company') within any description in paragraphs 1 to 4 would, if the holding company were a local authority, be under the control of that authority.

Provisions affecting regulated companies

Regulation 4 LACO (identification of companies)

A regulated company shall have mentioned on relevant documents the fact that it is a company controlled, or, as the case may be, influenced, by a local authority, within Part V LGHA; and naming the relevant authority or authorities. 'Relevant documents' mean business letters, notices and other company documents, being of any kind mentioned in paragraphs (a) to (d) of section 349 (1) CA.

Regulation 4 adds to the general requirements for company stationery as contained in section 349 and 351 CA. All company correspondence for a LACO regulated company must therefore state:
a) the name of the company
b) the company's place of registration and company number

c) the address of its registered office
d) the word 'limited' unless the company is exempted from this by section 30 CA.

Regulation 5 (requirements applicable to regulated companies)

LACO article 5 (1) – a regulated company shall not:
a) in respect of the carrying out of any related duty, pay to a regulated director remuneration in excess of the maximum amount
b) in respect of expenditure on travelling or subsistence in carrying out of any relevant duty, pay to a regulated director and allowance, or reimburse expenses, in excess of the maximum amount
c) publish any material which the relevant authority would be prohibited from publishing by section 2 Local Government Act 1986 (ie. material designed to affect public support for a political party).

LACO article 5 (2) – where a director becomes disqualified from membership of a local authority otherwise than being employed by a local authority or a controlled company, the company shall make such arrangements as may be necessary for a resolution to be moved for their removal in accordance with section 303 CA.

LACO article 5 (3):
a) for the purposes of paragraph (1) (a), the 'maximum amount' is the greatest amount which would for the time being be payable by the relevant authority in respect of a comparable duty performed on behalf of that authority
b) for the purpose of paragraph (1) (b), the maximum amount in relation to a director is the maximum amount of travelling or subsistence allowance which would for the time being be payable to that director by the local authority of which they are a member if the relevant duty were an approved duty for the purposes of section 174 Local Government Act 1972
c) 'regulated director' means a director of the company who is also a member of a relevant authority
d) 'relevant duty' means a duty carried out on behalf of the company.

LACO article 6 (provision of information to authority's auditor)

A regulated company shall provide, and authorise or instruct its auditors to provide:
a) to the person who is for the time being the auditor in relation to the accounts of the relevant authority, such information, and information about the affairs of the company as that person may require for the purpose of the audit of the local authority's accounts
b) to any person authorised by the Audit Commission, such information as that person or the Commission may require for the discharge of any function under Part III Local Government Finance Act 1982.

LACO article 7 (provision of information to local authority members)
1. Subject to paragraph (2), a regulated company shall provide to a member of a relevant authority such information about the affairs of the company as the member reasonably requires for the proper discharge of their duties.
2. Nothing shall require a company to provide information in breach of any enactment, or of any obligation owed to any person.

LACO article 8 (provisional of financial information to authority):
1. A regulated company shall, on the request of any relevant authority, provide to that authority, within such reasonable time as may be specified by the authority, such information about the affairs of the company as that authority may require for the purposes of an order for the time being in force under section 39 (revenue accounts and capital finance) LGHA.
2. Information required under paragraph (1) shall be supplied in such form as the relevant authority may reasonably require.

LACO article 9 (appointment of auditor)

A controlled company shall before it first appoints a person as auditor of the company, obtain the Audit Commission's consent to the appointment of that person.

Note that the Companies Act 1985 (Audit Exemption) Regulations 1994 (SI 1994/1935) and the Companies Act 1985 (Audit Exemption Amendment) Regulations 1994 (SI1994/2879) now exempt companies with an annual turnover not exceeding £350,000 from having to have accounts audited under the CA. However, these exemptions do not apply *inter alia* to parent companies or subsidiaries, and presumably not therefore to local authority controlled companies. The exemptions could conceivably apply to some influenced or minority interest companies.

Additional controls for local authority controlled companies which are not arm's length companies:

LACO article 10 (public inspection of minutes)
1. A controlled company which is not an arm's length company shall, until the expiry of four years beginning with the date of the meeting, make available for inspection by any member of the public a copy of the minutes of any general meeting of the company.
2 .Nothing in paragraph (1) requires a copy to be made available which includes any matter the disclosure of which would be in breach of any enactment, or of an obligation owed to any person.
3. Nothing in this article shall require a company to make available for inspection the minutes of any meeting before the date on which LACO came into force.

Regulated companies and capital finance

This is dealt with by Part V (articles 12 to 17 inclusive) LACO. Each local authority and its associated regulated companies are defined by article 12 as a 'local authority group'. In summary, article 13 and 14 LACO state that things done by or to a regulated company are treated as if they were done by or to the relevant local authority, and in respect of such things (other than a reduction in the company's liability) require the authority to have available an amount of credit cover.

Article 16 makes provision for determining a regulated company's liabilities, and article 17 governs internal dealings between the council and its own company. The detailed LACO provisions are as follows:

Article 13 (receipts, contracts and liabilities of regulated companies)
1. Subject to the following provisions of this article, where a regulated company on or after 1 April 1995:
   a) receives a sum which, if it were a local authority, would be a capital receipt
   b) receives consideration to which, if it were a local authority, section 61 would apply
   c) receives a sum by way of grant from a European Union institution to which, if it were a local authority, section 63 (4) would apply
   d) enters into a credit transaction
   e) with respect to a credit transaction, agrees to a variation of terms which, if it were a local authority, would be a variation within the meaning of section 51 (1)
   f) incurs additional liabilities within the meaning of article 16
   g) reduces its liabilities within the meaning of article 16
   the sum, consideration, credit transaction, variation, liabilities or reduction in question shall be treated for the purposes of the application of the Part IV LGHA as having been received, entered into, agreed, incurred, or, as the case may be, made by the relevant authority.

Paragraph (1) does not apply to any sum or consideration which apart from this paragraph, would fall within paragraph (1) if it is received by the company:
a) from a person who is a member of the same local authority group
b) in respect of the disposal of assets for charitable purposes.

Article 14 Application of Part IV LGHA: Requirement for credit cover
1. Where in relation to things done by or to a regulated company in a financial year (the 'current year') a relevant authority is treated by virtue of article 13 (1) as having:
   a) received a sum such as mentioned in article 13 (1) (a)

b) received any consideration as mentioned in article 13 (b)

c) received a sum such as mentioned in article 13 (1) (c)

d) entered into a credit transaction

e) agreed to a variation to the terms of a credit transaction

f) incurred additional liabilities

g) made a reduction in liabilities,

the provisions of Part IV LGHA shall apply to the members of the local authority group to the extent and subject to the modifications referred to in the following provisions of this article and in articles 15 to 18.

2. Subject to paragraph (4), with respect to each regulated company in the local authority group, Part IV shall apply subject to the modification that there is required to be available to the relevant authority in the financial year following the current year and amount of credit cover which is equal to the aggregate of:

a) the amount which, if the company were a local authority other than an authority to whom paragraph (3) below applies, the company would have been required to set aside as provision for credit liabilities in accordance with sections 59 or 61(4) with respect to sums or consideration falling within paragraph (1)(a) or (b) above

b) an amount equal to the total received by the company of sums falling within paragraph (1) paragraph (c) above

c) the amount which, if the company were a local authority, would be the initial cost of any credit transaction entered into by the company

d) the amount of credit cover which if the company were a local authority, would be required to be available to it in accordance with section 51 (4) with respect to any variations of the terms of a credit transaction

e) where in the current year the company incurs additional liabilities within the meaning of article 16, the amount of the excess referred to in article 16 (3).

3. This paragraph applies to a local authority which, at the beginning of the current year, had a credit ceiling of nil or a negative amount, and which has no money outstanding by way of borrowing other than: short term borrowing (within the meaning of section 45 (6)); borrowing which was undertaken under section 5 City of London (Various Powers) Act 1924; or borrowing undertaken before 24 August 1995, other than borrowing by the issue of stock on or after 15 December 1993 from a person who is not a relevant lender.

4. For the purposes of paragraph (2), an amount of credit cover shall only be required by a virtue of subparagraphs (c), (d) and (e) where the aggregate of the amounts referred to in those subparagraphs exceeds £10,000.

5. For the purposes of this article either of the following amounts, or both in any combination, constitutes an amount of credit cover:

a) an amount which the authority determined to set aside from the useable part of the authority's capital receipts or from a revenue account as provision to meet credit liabilities (being an amount over and above amounts required to be set aside by virtue of any other provision of Part IV)

b) an amount by which the authority determined to treat as reduced the balance of a credit approval.

6. In paragraph (5) (b):

a) a reference to a credit approval is a reference to a basic credit approval or a supplement to a credit approval issued or transferred to the authority and having effect to the financial year following the current year

b) the balance of a credit approval is that part of the approval with respect to which a determination has not been made under section 56 (1).

7. A determination by a local authority under paragraph (5) shall take effect at the time it is made, and shall be made not later than six months after the end of the financial year following the current year.

Article 15: Application of Part IV – increase in the basic credit approval

1. Where in a financial year ('the current year') a regulated company reduces its liabilities within the meaning of article 16, Part IV shall apply subject to the modification that the relevant authority may treat a relevant credit approval as increased by the amount relating to that company of the excess referred to in article 16 (4).

2. In paragraph (1), the reference to a relevant credit approval is a reference to a basic credit approval issued or transferred to the authority and having effect for the financial year following the current year.

3. A basic credit approval may be treated as increased under paragraph (1) notwithstanding that a determination has been made under section 56 (1) with respect to the whole or any part of the amount of the approval, and, where the amount of a basic credit approval is nil, the amount of the increase shall be treated as the amount of the approval.

Article 16 (liabilities of regulated companies)

1. Subject to para (6) any reference in this article to the relevant liabilities of a regulated company is a reference to the total of the company's liabilities less its current assets (and the total so calculated may, accordingly, be a negative amount); and for this purpose:

a) 'current assets' shall be construed in accordance with section 262 (1)CA, but do not include:

i) land in which the company has any interest

ii) any liability owed to the company by a member of the same local authority group unless the liability was incurred before the date on which the company became a regulated company ('the relevant date')

b) where the company's current assets in the financial year are reduced by the payments made by the company under:

i) any credit transaction treated as having been entered into by the relevant authority by virtue of article 13 (1) (d) above

ii) any variation of the terms of a credit transaction treated as having been agreed by the relevant authority by virtue of article 13 (1)(3) above,

they shall be treated as if those payments have not been made

bb) the company's current assets shall be treated as if they are not reduced by the defraying, after the relevant date, of expenditure which, if the company were a local authority, would be expenditure for capital purposes; provided that the total amount by which they may be treated as not reduced by expenditure shall not exceed the amount shown in the company's accounts on the relevant date as:

i) being available for capital expenditure – and

ii) having been reserved for that purpose out of income which if received by the authority, would have been revenue of the authority

c) 'liabilities' do not include:

i) any liability under a credit transaction entered into by a company after the relevant date

ii) any liabilities under an agreement entered into by the company after the relevant date to a variation of the terms to a credit transaction entered into before the relevant date

iii) any liability which is owed by the company to a person who is a member of the same local authority group, unless the liability was incurred before the relevant date

d) subject to paragraph (2), the sum of the called up share capital of a regulated company with respect to shares held by a person who is not a member of the same local authority group, and any premium paid to the company for such shares, is to be treated as a liability of the company.

2. Where any shares in a regulated company are transferred by the relevant authority to a person who is not a member of the same local authority group, the liabilities of the company on, and at any time after, the date on which the shares are transferred shall not include the amount which is on that date the called up share capital of the company with respect to those shares.

3. A regulated company incurs additional liabilities where in any financial year (referred to as 'year 2') its relevant liabilities exceed its relevant liabilities in the financial year immediately preceding year 2 (referred to as 'year 1').

4. A regulated company reduces its liabilities where its relevant liabilities in year 1 exceed its relevant liabilities in year 2.

5. In a financial year other than the last year, the relevant authority shall determine the relevant liabilities of a regulated company by reference to:

a) amounts shown for assets and liabilities in the company's balance sheet prepared as at a date in that year; or if there is more than one such balance sheet, in the last such balance sheet, or if there is no such balance sheet –

b) amounts which they determine to be assets and liabilities of the company on the last day of that year

i) In the last year, the relevant authority shall determine the relevant liabilities of a regulated company by reference to amounts which they determine to be assets and liabilities of the company on the day immediately before the day on which the company ceases to be a member of the same local authority group

ii) In paras (5a) and (5b) above, 'the last year' means the financial year in which the company ceases to be a regulated company or becomes a regulated company of a different local authority.

6. Where year 2 is the financial year in which the company becomes a regulated company, the amount determined by the relevant authority in accordance with paragraph (7) shall be treated for the purposes of paragraphs (3) and (4) as the company's relevant liabilities in year 1.

7. The relevant authority shall determine the amount by which the total of the company's liabilities as at the date immediately before the day on which the company became a regulated company exceeded the company's current assets at that date (and the total so calculated may, accordingly, be a negative amount); for this purpose:

a) 'current set' shall be construed in accordance with section 262(1) of the 1985 Act, but do not include land in which the company had any interest on that date; and

b) the sum of the called-up share capital of the company with respect to shares held on that date by persons who were not, on the following day, members of the same local authority group, and any premium paid to the company for such shares, is to be treated as a liability of the company.

8. Where two companies are members of the same local authority group, and the relevant liabilities of the companies in a particular financial year fall to be calculated at different dates as a result of a transaction or a group of transactions between those companies:

a) the relevant liabilities in that year of one company would, apart from this paragraph, be reduced

b) the relevant liabilities in that year of the other company would, if the relevant liabilities of the two companies fell to be calculated as at the same date, be increased

c) the relevant liabilities in that year of the other company are not increased or are increased by an amount which is less than the amount of reduction referred to in the subparagraph (a),

no account shall be taken of the amount of that reduction in calculating the relevant liabilities in that year of the company mentioned in the subparagraph (a).

Article 17 (dealings with members of a local authority group)

1. This paragraph applies where:

a) a local authority becomes the lessee under a lease of any property, and the lessor under the lease and the authority are members of the same local authority group

b) a local authority enters into a contract for the supply of any property, and the other party to the contract and the authority are members of the same local authority group

c) in either case, the property in question was acquired by the company after it became a regulated company.

2. Where paragraph (1) applies, the lease or the contract in question shall not be treated as a credit arrangement for the purposes of Part IV LGHA, and

any variation of such a lease or contract shall not be treated as a variation of such arrangement for those purposes.

3. Where a local authority received from a regulated company a sum which, apart from this paragraph, would be a capital receipt for the purposes of Part IV, the sum shall not be treated as a capital receipt for those purposes if the authority and the company are members of the same local authority group.

4. Where a local authority received from a regulated company any consideration which, apart from this paragraph, would fall within section 61 (1), section 61 shall not apply to the consideration if the authority and the company are members of the same local authority group.

Article 18 (provisions where there are two or more relevant authorities)

Article 18 applies to regulated companies which are controlled or influenced jointly by two or more local authorities.

Anything done by or to the regulated company shall be treated as having been done by or to each of the relevant participating authorities to the extent of its involvement in the company. The same applies where any provision in Part V LACO is imposed, or any entitlement conferred, on the relevant participating authority in relation to a regulated company, where the same requirement or entitlement shall be treated as having been imposed or conferred to the extent of that authority's involvement in the company.

The extent of each participating authority's involvement in the company is to be determined by agreement between the participating authorities, or in default of agreement, by a person, nominated jointly by such participating authorities, or where no such nomination can be agreed, by a person appointed by the secretary of state.

Section 31 Arbitration Act 1950 shall apply in the determination of any question by a person nominated or appointed as above.

Companies and the private finance initiative (PFI)

The Local Authorities (Capital Finance and Approved Investments) (Amendment) Regulations 1995 (SI1995/850), which came into force on 1 April 1995, are part of the government's private finance initiative and contain the following provisions relating to local authority companies.

Regulation 6 amends regulation 14 and schedule 1 Local Authorities (Capital finance) Regulations 1990. Its main effect is that the reserved part of a local authority's capital receipts shall be:

a) 25% in specified cases where a receipt is received between 1 April 1995 and 31 March 1996 in respect of a disposal of share capital or loan capital in a bus company or airport company

b) 50% in the case of a receipt from a disposal by a local authority of share or loan capital of which:

i) was acquired before 10 March 1988, or for the purpose of providing financial assistance under section 33 LGHA, and was issued by a company not concerned with the provision of housing or housing services

ii) is in a company formed by, or with the participation of, the authority for any of the purposes referred to in section 145 (1) Local Government Act 1972 (arts, entertainment etc)

iii) is in a waste disposal company formed by, or with the participation of, the authority.

Regulation 7 amends regulation 20 of the 1990 regulations so that where a local authority acquires shares in a company in return for the disposal of an asset, the reserved part of the notional capital receipt shall be nil if the asset was not acquired for housing purposes and if the expenditure on acquiring the asset would be expenditure for capital purposes.

Regulation 12 amends Part II schedule 4 to the 1990 Regulations so that in determining a local authority's adjusted credit ceiling, no account is taken of amounts set aside as credit cover under LACO.

CHAPTER 3

Types of Company

So far as local authorities are concerned the choice of corporate structure will normally be between: a company with a share capital, a company limited by guarantee, or an industrial and provident society registered under the Industrial and Provident Societies Act 1965.

Legislation and other surrounding circumstances will often dictate the particular type of corporate structure. In other cases the promoter may have several possible choices. The starting point is whether separate corporate status is required at all.

Running a company involves additional expense and administrative work, apart from the setting up costs. Company auditors will have to be appointed and paid for, in addition to a local authority's own audit controls. The company may require other advice and services which the council cannot provide to it directly, and which must be purchased externally. Local authority activities carried out through a company must not only comply with local government principles and constraints on spending and borrowing, but must also comply with CA and its associated regulations. An alternative solution which avoids the need to establish a separate corporate body will often be less complicated and more cost effective. Possible alternatives to a company might be:

- an unincorporated association without separate legal status
- a group or working party involving representatives of the council and other community or private organisations with a specific brief
- joint venture projects, many of which might be adequately dealt with under development agreement/leasing arrangements which do not require a company to be formed.

When corporate status is required the principle choices are as follow.

Company with a share capital

A company which will undertake any commercial enterprise for a profit will usually be registered under CA as a company limited by a share capital. This will enable the company to:

i)   limit the liability of its members to the value of their individual shareholding
ii) raise capital through the issue of shares
iii) transfer membership in the company simply through the sale of a member's shares
iv) provide a return on investment through the dividends on shares
v)   distribute capital and revenues amongst members on liquidation or otherwise.

Public and private companies

Share capital companies may exist as either private or public companies. Private companies are the simplest to form and administer and will be the norm for most local authority purposes. A public limited company is one which is registered as such and complies with the following requirements:

1. Its memorandum of association contains a clause stating that it is a public limited company and its name ends with the words 'public limited company' or 'plc' or its Welsh equivalent.
2. The memorandum must be in the form specified by Table F of the Company's (Tables A-F) Regulations 1985 (available from any law stationers).
3. The company must have an authorised share capital of at least £50,000.
4. Before starting business the plc must have allotted shares to the value of at least £50,000. Each allotted share must be paid up to at least one quarter of its nominal value together with the whole of any premium.
5. A newly formed plc cannot start business or borrow money until it has obtained a certificate to do so under section 117 CA from Companies House. To obtain this the company secretary or a director must swear a statutory declaration that the share capital requirements have been complied with. Details must also be supplied of the company's actual or estimated preliminary expenses and any benefits given to members.
6. A plc must have at least two directors. The company secretary must also be a person who appears to the directors, to have sufficient knowledge and ability to fulfil the statutory function and who has one of the following qualifications:
   a) they have held the office of secretary or assistant or deputy secretary on 22 December 1980
   b) for at least three of the preceding five years they were secretary of a non-private company
   c) they are a member of one of the following:
   Institute of Chartered Accountants of England and Wales, Institute of Chartered Accountants of Scotland, Chartered Association of Certified Accountants, Institute of Chartered Accountants of Ireland, Institute of Chartered Secretaries and Administrators, Institute of Cost and Management Accountants, or Chartered Institute of Public Finance and Accountancy

d) they are a barrister, advocate or a solicitor of any part of UK
e) they are a person who, from previous experience or membership of another body, appears to the director to be capable of discharging functions of secretary.

The advantages of a plc is that it has access to capital markets and can offer its shares for sale to the public through the stock exchange and can publish advertisements offering any of its securities to the public.

The downside is that a plc normally has only seven months after the end of its accounting reference period to deliver its accounts to Companies House, and it cannot take advantage of many of the provisions and exceptions available for smaller companies, neither can it qualify as a dormant company.

A private company with a share capital may re-register as a public company if its members pass a special resolution to do so and comply with relevant formal requirements and *vice versa*. However, a company limited by guarantee may not re-register as a public limited company.

Companies limited by guarantee

A company limited by guarantee will be the norm for a company formed to carry out a charitable or other non-profit making function, eg. a professional association or advisory group, city challenge or single regeneration budget partnership. Indeed only companies limited by guarantee can apply to the charity commission for charitable status.

The liability of each company member is limited to the amount which he has guaranteed (usually £1).

Industrial and Provident Societies (I & Ps)

Industrial and provident societies are not registered under CA but with the Registrar of Friendly Societies under the Industrial and Provident Societies Act 1965 as amended. I & Ps provide an alternative corporate structure for some community projects. Like CA companies, I & Ps have separate legal status and the benefit of limited liability.

A society qualifies for registration under the 1965 Act if:
a) it is a society for carrying on an industry, business or trade; and
b) it satisfies the registrar that either:
i) it is a *bona fide* co-operative society; or
ii) in view of the fact that its business is being or is intended on being conducted for the benefit of the community there are special reasons why it should be registered as an I & P rather than as a company under CA.

To qualify for registration otherwise than as a *bona fide* co-operative society, a society must satisfy the Registrar both that its business will be conducted for the benefit of the community and that there are special reasons why it should be so registered. A society must show among other things that it will benefit persons other than its own members and that its business will be in the interests of the community.

Typical societies which qualify for registration are housing associations. When considering whether organisations should be registered as I & Ps the Registrar will have regard to whether it is non-profit making and is prohibited by its rules from distributing its assets amongst its members, and to the following matters:

a) control of the society must under its rules be vested in its members equally and not in accordance with their financial interest in the society. In general the principle of 'one man, one vote' must apply

b) the rules must ensure that interest paid on share and loan capital will not exceed a rate necessary to obtain and retain the capital required to carry out the society's objectives. This rate may vary from time to time between societies of different classes and according to the term and security of loans

c) there must be no artificial restriction or membership with the object of increasing the value of proprietary rights and interests. Membership might, however, be limited by other physical characteristics.

European Economic Interest Groupings (EEIG)

European Economic Interest Groupings (EEIGs) were introduced by EEC Regulation 2137/85 and the European Economic Interest Groupings Regulations 1989 (SI 1989/638)

An EEIG is a form of association between companies, or other legal bodies, firms or individuals from different EU states who need to operate together across national frontiers. It is formed to carry out particular tasks for its members, and to facilitate or develop the economic activities for its members.

An EEIG has its own corporate status which is distinct from the individual businesses which make up its membership, and it can sign contracts and sue in its own name. However, it does not offer limited liability. It can be set in any member state and operate in any part of the EU, and can enter into arrangements with organisations outside the EU (although non-EU organisations cannot themselves join an EEIG).

The term 'economic activity' is widely defined and includes universities and research institutes, and participation by professional associations. For more information see guidance note CHN6 (March 1993) issued by Companies House.

34

Deciding which company to form

When deciding what form of corporate structure to set up, the basic questions are:
- whether it is to be a profit making or non profit making organisation
- what statutory constraints govern the choice of the company
- how the company will slot into the broader scheme of things.

Where express powers exist for the formation of a company, those powers will normally also stipulate the type of structure to be created and how it is to be managed.

In other cases, a particular corporate structure may be required to satisfy other statutory conditions. For example, a housing association must be set up either as an I & P or as a registered charity in order to qualify for registration under section 3 Housing Associations Act 1985. Without such registration, the housing association cannot receive direct financial assistance from a local authority. However, the types of company which may register as housing associations may be widened following proposals contained in government consultation paper: *More choice in the social rented sector* (published July 1995), which suggests that other non profit making companies should also be allowed to register.

Government white paper proposals contained in *Our future homes* (published June 1995) envisages the setting up of local housing companies to take over existing council housing stock. These organisations may or may not be profit making, but must be private sector led, with some council representation.

Local authority companies are not normally set up in isolation but as a part of the wider scheme – a vehicle to achieve a specific objective. In some cases, a share capital profit making company may be set up as the trading arm of a non-profit making organisation.

Charitable status

The only companies which can register for charitable status are the companies limited by guarantee. Charities enjoy tax and rating benefits and may be able to raise funds more easily from the public as well as from public sector grants. To qualify as a charity a company must have one of the following as its principal objectives:
- relief of the poor, aged or people with disabilities
- advancement of religion
- advancement of education
- other purposes which are beneficial to the community in a way which the

law regards as charitable. This last category is wide ranging and may include the following:

i) land and buildings for public use such as recreation grounds, parks, community or village halls, libraries and museums

ii) preservation of buildings and other objects of architectural or historic interest

ii) provision of facilities for people with disabilities

iv) protection of the environment and preservation of endangered species

v) resettlement and rehabilitation of offenders and drug abusers

vi) disaster relief

vii) animal welfare

viii) promotion of the arts.

As well as providing some financial benefits, registration as a charity also involves the following responsibilities:

a) a statement of account must be sent to the Charity Commission each year

b) a registered charity with an annual income of £10,000 (plus) must state on any documents appealing for funds and other financial documents, the fact that it is a registered charity

c) the Charity Commission must be informed of any changes to the memorandum or articles of association of a charitable company, and any changes to the registered details

e) if the charity ceases to exist, the Commission must be informed of this and be sent a copy of the company's final accounts and closing minutes

f) there are restrictions on the disposal of assets forming part of the permanent endowment of a charity.

Registration of a company with charitable status can take place at any time after the company has been formed, but it should be seen as a one way process. I & Ps cannot register with the Charity Commission but enjoy similar advantages.

CHAPTER 4

Formation of Companies

To register a company limited by share capital or guarantee, the following must be lodged at Companies House together with the registration fee (currently £20):

- memorandum of association – signed by each of the subscribers
- articles of association – signed by each of the subscribers
- form 10 – a statutory form containing details of the company name, registered office, the first directors and the company secretary. Page two of the form can be photocopied and used as an addendum sheet if there are more than two directors
- statutory declaration of compliance sworn by a director, secretary or a solicitor responsible for setting up the company and which confirms that all statutory formalities have been complied with.

It may be necessary to lodge additional documents if the company is to be exempted from using the word 'limited' in its name, or if the company name includes a word or expression regarded as sensitive. Volume 9 of the *Encyclopedia of forms and precedents* 5th Edition contains precedents of memoranda and articles of association for various company situations, although not specifically for local authority companies. Some adaptation of these precedents is therefore required.

CHN (18) (March 1993) sets out Companies House requirements as regards document quality. Section 706 CA allows the Registrar of Companies to reject documents which cannot be filmed satisfactorily. The registrar can then issue notice requiring the company to provide filmable quality documents within 14 days. To meet this standard, documentation must:

- be on paper which is white or otherwise of a background density not greater than 0.3
- documents must have a matt finish
- each page must be on A4
- each page must have a margin of at least 10mm wide. If the document is bound, the bound edge must have a margin of at least 20mm

- letters must be clear, legible and of uniform density
- letters and numbers must not be less than 1.8mm high, with a line width not less than 0.25mm
- letters and numbers must be black or otherwise providing reflecting line density of not less than 1.0.

So long as the paperwork is in order, Companies House will aim to process it and issue a certificate of incorporation within five working days. Companies House also offers a same day incorporation service at a cost of £200 compared to the standard £20.

On the receipt of a certificate of incorporation a private company can commence business.

Before taking steps towards company formation, the following issues should be addressed:
1. Define the purpose of the company and what powers it will require.
2. Who the members of the company will be.
3. What capital the company will need to raise.
4. Whether the council will require reserve powers.
5. What ancillary documentation will be required to enable the company to achieve its purposes, eg. a lease or management agreement between the company and the local authority.
6. Whether there is need for a formation agreement between the promoters before the company is set up.
7. What will happen to the company and its assets and liabilities after it has achieved its objective.

There are also several administrative considerations, namely:
8. Choosing a name.
9. Choosing a registered office.
10. Selecting the appropriate type of corporate structure.
11. Whether it should be set as a subsidiary or as a holding company.
12. The status of the new company under Part V LGHA and whether it will be regulated or unregulated under LACO.
13. Who should be the directors and how they should be appointed.
14. Who should be the company secretary.
15. What back-up services the company will require and how they should be provided.
16. Whether a prospectus will be issued if shares are to be offered to the public (this will only apply in the rare situation in which a local authority is participating in the formation of a plc).
17. Preparation of a business plan (an essential requirement if the company will be receiving funds on the government's single regeneration budget).

Memorandum and Articles of Association

The memorandum sets out the objectives and the powers of the new companies. The articles provide its constitution. While both documents are usually widely drawn, care must be taken to ensure that the company cannot do anything which might put the council, members or officers into an *ultra vires* situation, or which may contravene LGHA, LGCO or any other public sector legislation. Matters to be included in the memorandum of a share capital company are:

1. The name of the company (ending with the word limited, or as the case may be plc, unless the company is exempt from using the word limited or plc).
2. Whether the registered office is situated in England and Wales, or in Wales, or in Scotland.
3. The objects of the company.
4. That the liability of members is limited to the amount (if any) unpaid on shares held by them.
5. The amount of the authorised share capital and how this is to be divided. No subscriber may take less than one share and the memorandum must state how many shares each subscriber has agreed to take.

The memorandum for a guarantee company is similar to the above, save that there is no reference to a share capital. Instead each member undertakes to contribute an amount (usually limited to £1) towards the debts and liabilities of the company if it should be wound up.

The articles of association constitute a contract between the company and each of its members. Whereas the memorandum deals with powers and objectives, the articles are concerned with administrative matters, such as delegation, appointment and removal of directors, calling of meetings, issue of shares and payment of dividends.

The Companies (Tables A-F) Regulations 1985 SI805 as amended by SI1985/1052 set out a model form of articles of association on which a company limited by shares may rely instead of registering its own articles *(see Appendix)*. In other cases, relevant provisions of Table A can be incorporated into a company's articles by cross-reference.

Guarantee and other forms of company must each register articles in form of Table C, D or E, or as near to these forms as circumstances permit.

The articles of association of a local authority company may give the council extensive reserve powers as regards membership of the company and in the appointment and removal of directors. However, when drafting such reserve powers it must be noted:

1. A company whose articles reserve to the local authority a right to appoint or

remove a majority of directors will be a council controlled company for the purposes of section 68 (c) LGHA and therefore regulated under LGCO.

2. A company in which the council has more than a 20% stake, and a 'business relationship', and whose articles give the council the right to direct the company's operating and financial policies, will be under the council's 'dominant influence' and therefore regulated by LACO.

Name of company

A company may give itself any name so long as:
1. The particular name or similar name is not being used by another company.
2. The name does not include a sensitive word or expression unless permission has been obtained for this.
3. The name ends with the word 'limited' or as the case may be 'plc', unless the company has been exempted from this requirement.

A telephone call to Companies House will suffice to check whether a particular name is already in use. But it is not possible to reserve a particular name for future registration of a company.

CHN(2) and CHN(3) (published March 1993) set out examples of sensitive words or expressions for which prior approval is required. CHN(2) Appendix A lists certain words which require the approval of the Department of Trade and Industry because they imply:
● national or international connections, eg. International, English, Welsh
● government patronage and sponsorship, eg. Authority, Board, Council
● business pre-eminence or representative status, eg. Federation, Society, Institution
● specific objects or functions, eg. Charity, Patent, Cooperative, Chemist, Benevolent, Foundation.

For words within CHN(2) Appendix B, approval is also required but it is also necessary to ask the specific representative organisation whether it has any objection to the use of a particular word. For example, to use the word 'King' or 'Windsor' in a company name, it would first be necessary to write to the Home Office, A Division, Room 731, Queen Anne's Gate, London SW11 9H2. The fact that there might be an innocent explanation for the use of a particular word in a company name does not mean that approval will necessarily be given for its use.

A private company limited by guarantee may be exempted from using the word 'limited' in its name if its objective is the promotion of commerce, art, science, education, religion, charity or a profession, and its articles contain provisions that:
i) any profits or other income are to be spent in promoting the company's objects

ii) no dividends are to be paid to the members

iii) if the company is wound up, all the assets are to be transferred to another body which has similar objectives, or which promotes a charity.

To claim exemption it is necessary to lodge with the registration papers a statutory declaration in form 30 (5) (a).

Membership of company

The members of a share capital company are its shareholders. The Companies (Single Member Private Limited Companies) Regulations 1992 (SI 1699) (introduced 14 July 1992) allow a company to exist with only one member; a situation which might apply when a company or local authority sets up a wholly owned subsidiary company for which it is the sole subscriber.

Single re-generation budget and challenge fund companies

On 19 June 1995 the Department of the Environment issued a Guidance Note to regional government offices (GORs) explaining the steps which GOR staff should undertake when it is proposed that challenge fund grant should be paid direct to companies established for that purpose.

The over-riding concern is that arrangements to pay single-regeneration budget (SRB) challenge fund grant to companies should be prudent, safeguarding proprieties and providing for tight financial management. SRB companies are likely to fall into one of three categories:

i)   local authority companies regulated under LACO

ii) local authority unregulated companies (ie. which the council does not either control or have a dominant influence)

iii) private sector companies with no council participation (but possibly with other public sector bodies having a minority interest).

Companies regulated under LACO are effectively part of the local authority, and the SRB guidance is therefore related to local authority minority interest companies or companies to which there is no local authority involvement. Before releasing funds to such companies the GOR will wish to insure the following.

1. Company constitution

The objectives of companies established specifically to utilise SRB challenge fund monies should be consistent with approved bid and delivery plan, specifying the geographical area in which the company will operate, the activities in which it will be involved, and who will benefit from those activities. The memorandum of association must therefore:

a) limit the activities of the company to those which directly further SRB and related objectives, or are incidental to them. The memorandum should not include blanket provisions allowing the company to do anything which could be loosely linked to the achievement of the objective. An explicit statement must also be included that the company will not engage in speculative activities such as the trading of financial instruments

b) the investment of surplus monies should be limited to EU banks and building societies

c) the memorandum must limit the company's borrowing powers (other than in exceptional circumstances) to the borrowing set out in the business plan.

2. Articles of association

These must:

a) require borrowings to be approved by the board of directors and contain an overall cap on the level of company debt

b) prohibit any amendment of the memorandum or articles unless the proposal has been passed by at least 75% of membership.

3. Business plan and delivery plan

The company should have a business plan showing how it will mobilise resources to meet its objectives. If appropriate, this plan should be endorsed by independent accountants and must show that the company's capital base is robust and appropriate to its planned activities.

There should be a clear read across from the business plan to the agreed delivery plan. Therefore, the strategic objectives, activities, funding and outputs described in the SRB delivery plan are to be an integral part of the company's business plan. In some cases, the delivery plan may also serve as the business plan, with the addition of a cash flow forecast.

4. Board membership

The board should include non-executive directors with specific expertise matching the activities of the company, as well as representatives of the major parts in the scheme. However, such non-executive directors will not be nominated by GORs, to avoid the risk of the secretary of state being regarded in law as a shadow director, and thus exposed to unlimited liability and conflict of interests. It is a condition of challenge funds support that the company's management function should be adequately resourced in terms of both the numbers and the qualifications of key staff.

5. Offer letter

When replying to the challenge fund letter the company must indicate its willingness to sign a time limited funding agreement with the department, permitting the company to:

● claim payment in arrears

● provide adequate proof of expenditure supporting each claim

- provide to DOE auditors annually audited accounts and an updated business plan
- not revise the memorandum or articles without the required consent of the DoE while in receipt of SRB challenge funds support
- commit new or successor board members to obligations.

The purpose of these conditions is to obtain private sector assurance that the company is fit to receive public funding.

In exceptional cases the government may take the view that a company is worth supporting even if it doesn't satisfy each of the above checks.

The guidance notes also point out that the VAT situation has to be checked carefully, as direct payment of grant through companies may carry an additional liability for this as well as for corporation and income tax.

Forming an Industrial and Provident Society (I&P)
(see Chapter 3 for the criteria for registration as an I & P)

To register an I & P, the society must have at least seven founder members, unless its membership consists of two or more societies which themselves are already registered. The procedure is then to lodge with the Registrar of Friendly Societies:
- form A obtainable from the registrar and which must be completed with the names and addresses of the seven subscribers and the secretary
- two printed copies of the rules of society (in book form)
- the relevant fee.

The rules of the society must provide for all the matters required by schedule 1 of the Industrial and Provident Societies Act 1965.

The duplicate rule book must also be signed by each of the subscribers. The proposed name of the organisation must not be regarded by the registrar as undesirable.

Unless the society is adopting model rules which have already been approved by the registrar, rules should first be submitted to the registrar in draft form for preliminary examination. However, the registrar's acceptance of the rules only means that they conform to 1965 Act, not that they are necessarily prudent, clear and well-drafted.

The standard fee for registration of an I & P is £600 (as at 1 April 1995). However, this is reduced to £250 where model conditions are adopted.

Applications for I & P registration may be either made directly to the registrar or through one of the 24 promoting organisations listed on form F280 (available from the registrar). Each of these promoting organisations has its own model rules and specialisations. As well as promoting I & Ps, many of these organisations offer the alternative of a company limited by guarantee.

Registration as an I & P takes about two months, and on completion of registration a certificate will be issued.

Applying for charitable status

To establish a charity it is necessary to have a governing document. For a company limited by guarantee, the governing document is its memorandum and articles of association.

The Charity Commission has produced draft model governing documents for a trust deed, the constitution of an unincorporated association, and the memorandum and articles of a guaranteed company. These are available free of charge. Use of model conditions generally results in registration being completed more quickly.

As a first step towards registration as a charity it is necessary to complete a comprehensive questionnaire (form RE 96A) with details of the organisation's proposed name, objectives, activities, membership, finance, funding, tax treatment, trustees and paid staff. Enclosed with the completed questionnaire should be:
● two copies of the governing document (preferably in draft)
● minutes, newspaper cuttings and other literature
● copies of plans for the next 12 months
● copy of the long-term plan
● financial accounts
● copies of contracts with fundraisers
● accounts of any subsidiaries
● copy of conveyances, leases or tenancy agreements.

The Commission is prepared to consider a draft governing document and assess whether the proposed objects are charitable in law and the administrative provisions both adequate and appropriate. The Commission may also consult the Inland Revenue at this stage, as the Inland Revenue is entitled to object to registration of any organisation with charitable status.

The Commission will advise the promoters if changes are needed to the governing document. Only when the Commission is satisfied that the organisation and its activities are charitable, and has agreed to the wording of the governing document, will the organisation be invited to register as a charity.

CHAPTER 5

After Incorporation

First meeting of directors

As soon as possible after a certificate of incorporation has been issued by Companies House, the directors must hold their first board meeting. The issues to be resolved at this meeting are formal and include:

1. Record receipt of the certificate of incorporation and a copy of the memorandum and articles of association as registered.
2. Record the appointment of the first directors (as detailed on Form 10 lodged with the registration papers).
3. Appoint a person to chair the board of directors and to take the Chair at general meetings of the company.
4. Record the registered address of the company.
5. Record the appointment of the first company secretary.
6. Open a company bank account. The resolution required for this must be in the form the bank requires.
7. Appoint company auditors (noting that regulation 7 LACO requires auditors for regulated companies to be first approved by the Audit Commission).
8. Decide whether the company is to have a common seal and if so to adopt a design and lay down rules for its use and custody. A company is not now legally required to have a common seal; a deed signed by a director and secretary, or two directors, is sufficient for this purpose.
9. Appoint solicitors.
10. Make a formal allotment of shares.
11. Resolve to enter into any agreements or other documents between the company, the council, any private or voluntary sector partner, or any other third party, which is necessary to enable the company to fulfil the functions for which it was set up. This may include employment contracts in relation to staff taken over.
12. Instruct the company secretary to forward the appropriate forms to Companies House
13. Approve insurance arrangements.

As soon as possible after the first board meeting, the company secretary must:

1. Complete and send the relevant statutory forms to Companies House.
2. Write the minutes of the meeting. The minutes of the company must be kept separate from the council minutes, and must be signed by the Chair of the meeting. The company can only do what it has been authorised to do by resolution.
3. Open the company bank account and notify auditors, solicitors and other professional service providers to the company.
4. Arrange for the transfer of share capital from the council (if it is a shareholder) and other participants who have agreed to purchase shares in the company.
5. Issue the relevant share certificates – each to be signed by the director and the secretary.
6. Make up a company file containing the following statutory registers:
   a) a register of members (providing details of each member's shareholding if applicable)
   b) a register of directors
   c) a register of secretaries
   d) a register of directors' interests
   e) a register of charges (whether fixed or floating).
   Registers may be kept on computer instead of book form, so long as the details can be printed out as hard copy.
   The statutory registers of a company can be obtained from the Solicitor's Law Stationery Society (OYEZ) or other law stationers. If the statutory registers are kept otherwise than at the registered office of the company, Companies House must be notified of this.
7. Put into place any agreements and other documents authorised by company resolution as being necessary to enable the company to do what it was set up to do. Such documents might include:
   a) a service level agreement between the company and the council or other participants
   b) employment contracts
   c) leasing of accommodation
   d) arrangements between the council or other third parties for payroll or other administrative back-up services.

Functionaries and their duties

Directors

The term 'director' includes any person carrying out similar duties, but under a different name, eg. 'trustee', 'executive committee member'.

A director has a combined role as a trustee of the company's assets, agent

46

for the company in that their actions will bind the company so far as they act within the scope of their authority; and someone who is responsible for the day to day management of the company. A director as such is not an employee of the company, but may be employed by the company in some other capacity.

The first directors of the company are those named in Form 10. Replacement or additional directors are then appointed either by existing directors or by shareholders in accordance with the articles of association. A director is not personally required to hold shares in the company, unless the articles so provide.

A person will cease to be a director if:
a) their term of office expires without renewal
b) they resign
c) the members of the company at a general meeting resolve to terminate their employment. This is a statutory shareholder's right, notwithstanding any contract or articles to the contrary. Termination of a director's office in this way is without prejudice to any claims which they may have against the company resulting from any termination of their employment
d) if they become bankrupt (unless they are permitted to carry on as a director by the court)
e) they are disqualified following conviction of an offence related to CA legislation
f) in the case of a regulated company, they are prevented from being a director by article 5 (a) LACO (where a director is disqualified from membership of a local authority). A resolution must then be passed for their removal).

A director is not entitled to remuneration unless the articles of association so provide. For companies regulated by LACO, remuneration is further restricted by article 5 (3).

A director may not delegate duties to another person unless the articles so provide, or such power is included in their terms of appointment. Table A (articles 65-69) provides for the appointment of alternate directors.

Disclosure under section 317 CA

A director who is personally interested in a contract or a proposed contract with a company must disclose their interest either:
● at the first board meeting when the contract is first considered or
● at the first board meeting after they acquired an interest in the contract.

A general notice to the directors to the effect that:
i) they are a member of a specified company or firm and are to be regarded as interested in any contract which may, after the date of the notice be made with that company or firm

47

ii) they are to be regarded in any contract, which may, after the date of the notice, be made with a specified person who is connected with them,

shall be deemed to be sufficient declaration of interest in relation to any such contract, provided that no such notice shall be effective unless either it is given at a meeting of directors, or the director takes reasonable steps to ensure that it is brought up and read at the next meeting of directors after it is given.

Shadow directors

For purposes of section 741 CA, a shadow director is a person in accordance with whose directions or instructions the directors of a company are accustomed to act. However, this does not apply, if that person's directions or instructions are only given in a professional capacity, such as a solicitor or accountant. Neither will a holding company be a shadow director of any of its subsidiaries by reason only of this section. A shadow director is treated as a director of the company and is subject to provision requiring declaration of interest.

Executive and non-executive directors

These are non-statutory terms. A full-time working director is 'executive', while a person who devotes only part of their time to company business is a 'non-executive' director. Councillor/directors will mostly be non-executive.

Managing director

Article 84 Table A allows directors to appoint a person to be 'managing director', and to delegate any of their powers and fix remuneration.

Company secretary

If it is the directors who make the policy decisions for the company. It is the secretary who is its chief executive officer. Every company is required to have a company secretary, and it is usual for them to be someone other than the directors of the company. However, there would seem to be nothing to stop a director acting also as a secretary of the company so long as they are not the sole director of the company. A company secretary is an officer of the company and subject to the same financial penalties for breaches of company regulations as the directors.

CHAPTER 6

The Company and its Relationship with Others

The company and third parties

To protect the interests of third parties dealing with a company in good faith, sections 35, 35A and 35B CA (implementing European Council Directive EEC-68-151) state:

Section 35 (a company's capacity not limited by its memorandum)
1. The validity of an act done by a company shall be called into question on the ground of lack of capacity by reason of anything in the company's memorandum.
2. A member of a company may bring proceedings to restrain the doing of an act which but for subsection (1) would be beyond the company's capacity; but no such proceedings shall lie in respect of an act to be done in fulfilment of a legal obligation arising from a previous act of the company.
3. It remains the duty of the directors to observe any limitations on their powers flowing from the company's memorandum; and action by the directors which but for subsection (1) would be beyond the company's capacity may only be ratified by the company by a special resolution.
   A resolution ratifying such action shall not affect any liability incurred by the director or another person; relief from any such liability must be agreed to separately by a separate resolution.
4. The operation of this section is restricted by section 30B (1) of the Charities Act 1960 [now section 65 Charities Act 1993] and section 112 (3) of the Companies Act 1989 in relation to companies which are charities; and section 322A below (invalidity of certain transactions to which directors or their associates are parties) has effect notwithstanding this section.

Section 35A (power of directors to bind the company)
1. In favour of a person dealing with a company in good faith, the power of the board of directors to bind the company, or authorise others to do so, shall be

49

deemed to be free of any limitation under the company's constitution.

2. For this purpose:

a) a person 'deals with' a company if they are a party to any transaction or other act to which the company is a part of

b) a person shall not be regarded as acting in bad faith by reason only of their knowing that an act is beyond the powers of the directors under the company's constitution

c) a person shall be presumed to have acted in good faith unless the contrary is proved.

3. The references above to limitations on director's powers under the company's constitution include limitations deriving from:

a) a resolution of the company in general meeting or a meeting of any class of shareholders

b) any agreement between the members of the company or of any class of shareholders.

4. Subsection (1) does not affect any right of the member of a company to bring proceedings to restrain the doing of an act which is beyond the powers of a director; but no such proceedings shall lie in respect of an act to be done in fulfilment of an obligation arising from a previous act of a company.

5. Nor does that subsection affect any liability incurred by the director, or any other person, by reason of the director exceeding their powers.

6. The operation of this section is restricted by section 30 (B) (1) of the Charities Act 1960 [now section 65 of the 1993 Act] and section 112 (3) of the Companies Act 1989 in relation to companies which are charities; and section 322 E below (invalidity of certain transactions to which certain directors or their associates are parties) has effect notwithstanding this section.

Section 35 B (no duty to inquire as to capacity or authority of directors)

A party to a transaction with a company is not bound to enquire about whether it is permitted by the company's memorandum or about any limitation on the powers of the board of directors to bind the company or authorise others to do so.

It will be seen that section 35A and 35B CA are subject to several statutory exceptions. These are:

Section 65 Charities Act 1993 replacing section 35 B (1) Charities Act 1960 (invalidity of certain transactions) which states:

1. Sections 35 and 35A of the Companies Act 1985 (capacity of the company not limited by its memorandum; power of directors to bind company) do not apply to the acts of the company which is a charity except in favour of a person who:

a) gives full consideration on money or money's worth in relation to the act in question

50

b) does not know that the act is not permitted by the company's memorandum or as the case may be is beyond the powers of its directors
c) who does not know at the time the act is done that the company is a charity.
2. However, where such a company purports to transfer or grant an interest in the property, the fact that the act was not permitted by the company's memorandum or, as the case may be, that the directors in connection with the act exceeded any limitations on their powers in the company's constitution, does not affect the title of the person who subsequently acquires the property or any interest in it for full consideration without actual notice of any such circumstances affecting the validity of the company's act.
3. In any proceedings arising from subsection (1) above the burden of proving:
a) that a person knew that the act was not permitted by the company's memorandum or was beyond the powers of the directors
b) that a person knew that the company was a charity, lies on the person making that allegation.
4. Where a company is a charity, the ratification of an act, to which section 35 (3) Companies Act 1985, or the ratification of a transaction to which section 322A of that act applies (invalidity of certain transactions to which directors or their associates are parties), is ineffective without the prior written consent of the Commissioners.

While the above provisions provide general commercial protection to a person dealing with a company in good faith against any deficiencies in its memorandum or articles of association, it is unclear the extent to which they protect a person dealing with local authority companies. The general rule of local government is that innocent third parties have no protection when a local authority acts beyond its powers, as was demonstrated in *Credit Suisse v Allerdale Borough Council*.

But it must be noted that in the Allerdale case it was not the company itself which was being sued but the council personally under its loan guarantee.

If a LACO regulated company acts in a manner which is *ultra vires*, then probably so also has the local authority which controls or influences it. Does this then leave third parties without remedy?

The validity of an act done by a local authority company is limited not only by the company's own memorandum and articles, but by LACO (if applicable) and public law generally. Section 35 only protects third parties against deficiencies in the memorandum, not against general breaches of the law.

In the case of a LACO regulated company, third parties should have express notice of its status, as letterheads and other company documents are required by LACO to disclose this.

For an unregulated company in which the council has a minority interest and no dominating influence, these disclosure requirements will not apply. There are arguments for saying that sections 35, 35A and 35B give greater protection to third parties dealing with unregulated companies, than for LACO regulated companies.

Even if a third party is protected by sections 35, 35A and B against the *ultra vires* activities of a LACO regulated company, any expenditure incurred by the company will remain 'unlawful expenditure' for the purposes of section 70 LGHA, and the Audit Commission may proceed against the person responsible for incurring it.

CHAPTER 7

The Company and the Local Authority

Delegation of functions

The power of a local authority to delegate any of its decision making functions to a company would seem to be precluded by section 101 Local Government Act 1972, which allows a council to delegate its functions only to a committee, sub-committee, an officer of the local authority or to another local authority. This does not prevent the company from contracting to provide investigative or other bureaucratic services to the local authority, short of actual decision making.

In *R v Hertsmere Borough Council ex p Woolgar, The Times, 10 May 1995*, it was held in the High Court that a council could delegate to a registered housing association the bureaucratic process of investigating, reporting back and making recommendations on applications made to the council by people claiming homelessness, so long as the council's decision making function itself was not delegated.

Section 70 Deregulation and Contracting Out Act 1994 now allows the secretary of state to make orders delegating specific local authority functions to such persons or organisations as he may stipulate by a statutory instrument.

Conceivably, functions might be delegated to a local authority company by an order under this section. Section 70 (1) applies to any local authority function which:
a) is conferred by any enactment; and
b) by virtue of section 101 Local Government Act 1972 or section 56 Local Government (Scotland) Act 1973 (arrangements for discharge of functions by Local Authorities) may be exercised by an officer of the authority
c) which is not excluded by section 71 below.

Section 70 (3) requires the minister first to consult such representatives of local government as may be considered appropriate before making contracting out functions under section 70.

Section 71 excludes the secretary of state from contracting out under section 70 any local authority functions if:
a) its exercise would constitute the exercise of jurisdiction of any court or any tribunal which exercises the judicial power of the state
b) its exercise or a failure to exercise, would necessarily interfere with or otherwise affect the liberty of any individual
c) it is a power or right of entry, search or seizure into or of any property
d) it is a power to make subordinate legislation.

Under section 72 of the 1994 Act anything done or omitted to be done by any person or organisation to which functions have been delegated will, in the case of local authority functions, be treated as having been done or omitted to be done by the relevant local authority.

Schedules 15 and 16 of the 1994 Act contain provisions supplementary to section 70.

Schedule 15 contains provisions modifying restrictions on the disclosure of information where functions of ministers or officers of local authorities are contracted out.

Schedule 16 contains other provisions relating to the contracting out of functions whether under section 69 or section 70.

As regards the scope of a statutory instrument delegating the relevant functions, sections 69 (4) and (5) state as follows:
4) "An order under this section may provide that a function to which this section applies may be exercised, and an authorisation given by virtue of such an order may (subject to the provisions of the order) authorise the exercise of such a function:
a) either wholly or to such extent as may be specified in the order or authorisation
b) either generally or in such cases or areas as may be specified
c) either unconditionally or subject to the fulfilment of such conditions as may be so specified".
5) "An authorisation given by virtue of an order under this section:
a) shall be for such period, not exceeding 10 years, as is specified in the authorisation
b) may be revoked at any time by the minister or office holder [or local authority] by whom the authorisation is given
c) shall not prevent that minister or office holder [or local authority] or any

other person from exercising the function to which the authorisation relates".

Back-up services

A newly established company will require somewhere to operate from, legal and accounting advice, and administrative, payroll and secretarial back-up.

The extent to which a council can provide these services directly to a local authority company is limited by the Local Authorities (Goods and Services) Act 1970, which allows councils to provide certain categories of services to other local authorities or organisations having 'public body status' as defined by section 1 (4) of the 1970 Act. The services which the councils may then provide are:
a) the supply by the authority to the body of any goods or materials
b) the provision by the authority for the body of administrative, professional or technical services
c) the use by the body of any vehicle, plant or apparatus belonging to the authority and, without prejudice to paragraph (b) the placing at the disposal of the body of the services of any person employed in connection with the vehicle or other property in question
d) the carrying out by the authority of works of maintenance in connection with the land or buildings for the maintenance of which the body is responsible.

Also a local authority may acquire and store any goods or materials which in their opinion they may require for the purposes of paragraph (a) above.

But nothing in paragraphs (a) to (c) above authorises a local authority either to construct any building or works, or to be supplied with any property or provided with any service except for the purposes of functions conferred on the authority otherwise than by the 1970 Act. Any agreement made between the authority and the body concerned may contain such terms as to payment or otherwise, as the parties consider appropriate.

A local authority housing action trust established under Part III Housing Act 1988 automatically has public body status for the purposes of the 1970 Act. The Secretary of State for the Environment may also, by statutory instrument, declare other named organisations exercising functions of a public nature to be 'public bodies'. Many voluntary and public sector organisations as well as some city challenge projects have already been granted this status.

Section 2 states that the 1970 Act adds to and does reduce any other statutory or incidental power allowing a council to provide goods and services to third parties.

In appropriate cases it may be beneficial to seek 'public body status' for a local authority company under the 1970 Act. In the first instance, enquiry should be made to Local Government 2 Division (LG2), Department of the Environment, Room P1/139A, 2 Marsham Street, London SW1P 3EB; Tel: 0171-276 4102; Fax: 0171-276 4099/4103. But the criteria is strict.

The secretary of state will only consider applications for public body status from an organisation which can demonstrate that it is:
a) non-profit making
b) performing functions a local authority is also empowered to undertake, or closely linked to the authority
c) performing functions of a public nature
d) not in direct competition with the private sector.

In addition:
e) the services to be provided by the local authority must not be available elsewhere in the private sector
f) the benefit to the public must outweigh the detriment to the private sector.

If satisfied that the company meets the above criteria, and that public body status ought to be granted, the secretary of state will make the necessary statutory instrument and lay it before parliament.

Where the 1970 Act applies, services will normally be provided by the council to the company on a commercial arm's length basis. However, where public body status cannot be obtained, the company must buy in its own ancillary services independent of the local authority.

Land

Section 123 Local Government Act 1972 (as amended) will apply to any disposal or leasing of land from the council to the company. Unless it is a tenancy not exceeding seven years, the disposal must be at arm's length and at best consideration. If the land is public open space (or similar) or has charitable status, the relevant statutory formalities must be complied with on its disposal. The fact that a company occupies council land at an undervalue is a determining factor in deciding whether there is a 'business relationship' for the purposes of Part V LGHA.

The company and its employees

The Transfer of Undertakings (Protection of Employment) Regulations 1981 (TUPE) may apply to staff transferred from the local authority to the company (other than staff remaining within the council's employ but who are seconded to company duties).

Care must be taken in the transfers of service tenancies as the Housing Act 1985 only relates to council service tenancies. Company service tenancies will fall within the Housing Act 1988 which contains material differences to the 1985 Act regime.

Public procurement

A council which buys in goods and services whether from its own company or from elsewhere must comply with relevant tendering and other public procurement requirements so far as they are relevant to the particular transaction.

CHAPTER 8

Insurance and Risk

Matters a company should be insured for are:
- employers and public liability
- professional indemnity insurance (if the company will be providing advice or other services to third parties or the public generally)
- libel (if the company will be publishing literature)
- buildings and contents insurance (if the company owns or leases premises or equipment).

In addition, directors and officers of the company should consider what insurance they themselves require to cover any personal risk incidental to their appointments. The definition 'officers' of a company, is normally taken to include the directors, secretary and other senior management.

While officers acting in good faith within the powers of the company will normally be protected by the company's limited liability status, circumstances may arise when they can be held personally liable to the company, its shareholders or to third parties. Officers who are also councillors or council employees run a double risk in that they can also be held personally liable under the Local Government Finance Act 1982 at the suit of the council's own district auditor for public expenditure which has been unlawfully incurred. Otherwise the circumstances under which an officer of a limited liability company can be held personally liable are:
a) breach of fiduciary duty – a company director is under a duty to act in good faith and in the best interests of the company
b) acting outside the powers of the company
c) if it is not made clear to third parties, in correspondence or otherwise, that the officer is acting as an agent of a limited liability company. Therefore cheques and other stationery must bear the full name of the company and comply with other CA requirements
d) if a director gives a personal guarantee in respect of a company liability
e) if a local authority councillor or employee, who is also an officer of an associated company, fails to make clear to a third party the capacity in which

they are acting (whether they are an agent for the council or for the company), or if they commit the council to incurring or guaranteeing company expenditure without lawful authority. It is conceivable that they would then incur personal liability under the Local Government Finance Act 1982

f) liability for negligence; in this respect, officers who are appointed because of a particular specialisation (such as council lawyer or accountant) will owe a higher duty of care than a lay councillor/director.

Personal liabilities may also arise where a company goes into insolvent liquidation in circumstances where an officer can be shown to have acted in bad faith. Relevant statutory provisions are:

Section 213 Insolvency Act 1986 fraudulent trading (summary)

If in the course of the winding up of the company it appears that any business of the company has been carried out with intent to defraud creditors, or for any fraudulent purpose, then the court on the application of the liquidator may declare that any persons who were knowingly parties to the carrying on of the business in this manner are liable to such contribution (if any) to the company's assets as the court thinks proper.

Section 214 Insolvency 1986 (Wrongful trading) (summary)

1. If during winding up of a company it appears that subsection (2) below applies in relation to any person who is or has been a director of the company, the court, on the application of the liquidator, may consider that person to be liable to make such contribution (if any) to the company's assets as the court thinks proper.
2. This subsection applies in relation to any person if:
   a) the company has gone into insolvent liquidation
   b) at some time before the commencement of the winding up of the company, that person knew or ought to have concluded that there was no reasonable prospect that the company would avoid going into insolvent liquidation
   c) that person was a director of the company at that time.
   The court shall not make a declaration under section 214 in any case where the time mentioned above was before 28 April 1986.
3. The court shall not make a declaration under this section with respect to any person if it satisfied that after the condition specified in subsection (2) (b) was first satisfied in relation to them, that the person took every step to minimise the potential loss to the company's creditors which he ought to have taken.
4. For the purposes of subsection (2) and (3), the facts which a company director ought to know and ascertain, the conclusions which they ought to reach and the steps which they ought to take are those which would be known, ascertained, reached, taken, or followed by a reasonably diligent person having:

a) the general knowledge, skill and experience that will reasonably be expected of a person carrying out the same functions as are carried out by the director in relation to the company

b) the general, skill and experience that that director has.

5. The reference in subsection (4) to the functions carried out in relation to a company by a director of the company includes any functions which they do not carry out but which have been entrusted to them.

6. For the purposes of this section a company goes into insolvent liquidation if it goes into liquidation at a time that its assets are insufficient for the payment of its debts and other liabilities and the expenses of the winding up.

7. In this section 'director' includes a shadow director.

8. This section is without prejudice to section 213.

It should be noted that where a court makes a declaration either under section 213 or section 214 that a person is liable to make a contribution to the company's assets, the court may make a disqualification order against that person, whether or not an application for such an order is made by any person (Company Director Disqualification Act 1986 section 10).

An officer of a company who is sued for negligence, default, breach of duty or breach of trust may seek relief from the court under section 727 CA. Such relief may be given if the court is satisfied that the officer has acted honestly and reasonably and that having regard to the circumstances of the case (including those connected with their appointment) they ought fairly to be excused either wholly or in part on such terms as the court thinks fit. Such relief may be sought under section 727 (2) even if civil proceedings against the officer have not yet begun, if the officer has reason to believe that they will be sued.

Where a director is paid for their services the court may be less disposed to give them relief than it would for a person acting gratuitously.

Section 310 CA renders void any provision in a company's articles or in a contract with the company which purports to indemnify any officer or auditor of the company against any liability attaching to them for negligence, default, breach of duty or breach of trust of which they may be guilty in relation to the company. But the articles of association can lawfully indemnify an officer or auditor against costs incurred, *inter alia*, in defending any proceedings whether civil or criminal in which judgment is given in their favour, or which they are acquitted.

Insurance

There are only a few insurance companies offering cover against directors and officers liability, and premiums can be expensive.

As a first step when arranging insurance for a council owned or influenced company it is prudent to clarify the extent of insurance cover which may already exist either:
i) under the council's own insurance policy
ii) under the insurance of any other organisation participating in the company.

In cases where a local authority is providing advice or services directly to an associated company it is important to clarify whether council staff providing such advice or assistance are providing their services as part of their work for the council (in which case they should be covered by the council's own insurance), or whether they are working for the company. If in doubt, the council's insurer should be asked to provide a written confirmation as to the insurance position.

An example of a directors and officers liability insurance policy is that offered by Sun Alliance. Their policy is split into three parts namely:
1. *Directors and officers liability section:* covering legal liability of directors and officers for wrongful acts arising from breach of contract, trust, duty, act omission etc., committed in their capacities as directors or officers as trustees of the company's pension fund.
2. *Company reimbursement section:* indemnifying the company against payments which it is lawfully permitted to make in respect of claims made against directors and officers which would otherwise have been subject to indemnity under the directors and officers liability section above.
3. *Representation expenses extension:* for representation expenses incurred by directors and officers and the company in connection with an official investigation into the company's affairs, or the prosecution of any director or officer arising out of any wrongful act.

The policy contains exclusions for dishonesty, death, illness or injury, penalties, breach of professional duty, pollution, intentional breaches of contract etc.

Where there are subsidiary companies it is usual for the policy to be issued on behalf of the holding company, on the basis that it will include directors and officers of subsidiaries. Quotations can usually be given with or without an excess.

The Sun Alliance policy is written on a 'claims made' basis, meaning that it applies to claims notified to the insurer during the period of insurance. It is therefore essential that insurance cover is maintained as long as the possibility of a claim being made exists. Former directors and officers remain liable for claims arising for occurrences which took place prior to their retirement.

CHAPTER 9

Exit Procedures, meetings and Audit

Exit procedures

What is to happen once the company has achieved its purpose? Suppose the project becomes abortive and the council wishes to pull out. What if a joint venture partner defaults?

When putting a scheme together, these possibilities must be taken into account and appropriate exit procedures put into place. Exit procedures for a solvent company might be:

- in the case of a joint venture company, for one of the partners to buy out the shares of the other
- in the case of a share capital company, the sale of the company and its assets to a third party
- a transfer of the assets of the company to the council or another successor body
- a member's voluntary winding up under section 84 Insolvency Act 1986, *inter alia*, following a special resolution (ie. a resolution passed with the three quarters majority at a general meeting of which not less than 21 days prior notice has been given specifying the proposed resolution). Before there can be a voluntary resolution to wind up a limited company, the directors must first make a statutory declaration to the effect that they have made a full inquiry into the company's affairs and are of the opinion that the company will be able to pay its debts in full and interest within such period (not exceeding 12 months) as the declaration may specify (section 89 Insolvency Act 1986).

This declaration must be delivered to Companies House within 15 days from the date the resolution to wind up the company is passed. Notice must also be published in the *London Gazette* within 14 days of passing the winding up resolution. The company will then appoint a liquidator to wind up the affairs of the company, pay its debts, and distribute surplus assets.

- by striking off – this is a new procedure introduced by section 31 (1) and schedule 5 Deregulation and Contracting Out Act 1994 (adding new sections 652A to 652F to CA and amending section 653 CA). The changes, which took effect on 1 July 1995 now allow directors of private non-trading companies to apply to Companies House for the removal of the company from the Companies Register. The procedure requires completion of a new form 652a and payment of a £10 fee.

A company is eligible for striking off under these new provisions if it has not traded or otherwise carried on business within the preceding three months, or changed its name, or disposed of trading assets, or engaged in any activity other than one necessary or expedient for making a striking off application, settling the company's affairs or meeting a statutory requirement.

Within seven days of Form 652a being lodged at Companies House, copies of the form must be provided to each member of the company as well as to employees, managers or trustees of any employee pension fund, other directors who have not signed the form and the relevant VAT office.

On receiving a completed Form 652a, Companies House will check it, put it on the company record and acknowledge it. The Registrar of Companies must also advertise the striking off application in the *London Gazette* and allow at least three months for objections.

However a company is dissolved, any assets which have not been transferred out of the company beforehand will vest in the crown as *bona vacantia*.

Meetings

Annual general meeting

Section 366 CA requires each company to hold an annual general meeting (AGM) in each year and within 15 months of the previous AGM. The first AGM must be held within 18 months of incorporation.

Section 366A CA (as amended) allows a private company to pass an 'elective resolution' to dispense of the holding of AGMs. Such elective resolution must be made with accordance of section 397A CA and must be carried unanimously. Any company member has the right at any time to serve notice requiring an AGM to be called.

Section 381A CA (as amended) introduces a written resolution procedure for private companies. Any resolution which can be passed at a general meeting, or by a meeting of a particular class of members, can now be done without a meeting, so long as a written resolution has been signed by or on on behalf of all of the company members who would have been entitled to attend the meeting and vote.

A copy of the original resolution must be sent out to the company's auditors under section 381B. If the resolution concerns the auditors as auditors, they may within seven days give notice to the company stating that in their opinion the resolution should be considered by the company in a general meeting, or as the case may be by a meeting of the relevant class of members.

A written resolution under section 381A shall not take effect unless the auditors notify the company that it does not concern them as auditors; or it does concern them but need not be considered at a meeting, or the seven day period expires without notice from the auditors.

Extraordinary general meetings

Any general meeting other than an AGM is called an extraordinary general meeting (EGM). EGMs may be called by the directors at any time. Members holding between them at least one tenth of the paid up capital of the company can requisition an EGM. On receiving such a requisition directors must within 21 days give notice convening the meeting, which must then be held within 28 days thereafter.

Section 380 CA lists certain types of resolution which have to be notified to Companies House and attached to copies of the articles of association issued after the resolution has been passed.

Accounting and audit requirements

The directors of a limited company are responsible for maintaining proper accounting records and preparing financial statements which give a true and fair view and have been prepared in accordance with CA. Directors are also responsible for making available to the company auditors, as and when required, all the company's accounts and records and all other related information, including minutes of all managers and shareholders meetings.

Company auditors have a statutory responsibility to report to the members of the company whether in their opinion the financial statements give a true and fair view of the state of the company's affairs and of the profit or loss of the year and whether they have been properly prepared in accordance with CA. In arriving at their opinion, the auditors are required to consider the following matters, and to report on any respect on which the auditors are not satisfied:
a) whether proper accounting records have been kept by the company and proper returns adequate for audit have been received

b) whether the company's balance sheet and profit and loss account are in agreement with the accounting records and returns

c) whether the auditors have obtained all the information and explanations which they think necessary for the purposes of audit

d) whether the information in the director's report is consistent with that in the audited and financial statement.

In addition, there may be other matters which need to be dealt with in the auditor's report. For example, if the financial statements do not give full disclosure of the directors' remunerations or of their transactions with the company, CA requires the auditors to disclose such matters in their report.

Auditors also have a professional responsibility to report if the financial statements do not comply in any material respect with accounting standards, unless in their opinion the non-compliance is justified in the circumstances and are adequately disclosed.

Audits must be conducted in accordance with auditing standards issued by the accountancy bodies and have regard to relevant auditing guidelines.

Ultimate responsibility for the prevention and detection of irregularities and fraud rests with the directors. But auditors should plan their audits so they have a reasonable expectation of detecting material mistakes in the financial statements or accounting records resulting from irregularities or fraud. Such examinations should be relied upon to disclose irregularities and frauds which may exist.

Corporation tax

Auditors should prepare corporation tax computations based on the business accounts for each financial period, and submit and agree these with the Inland Revenue. The company should then be advised on its liability to corporation tax and of the due date of payment.

Auditors should review Inland Revenue assessments, lodge any appeals which may be necessary, and advise the company in connection with the payment of tax.

Directors should sign an appropriate authority allowing the Inland Revenue to send to the auditors copies of relevant assessments and must in any case forward immediately on receipt, all assessments and copies of other communications received from the Inland Revenue. Directors are legally responsible for the completion and submission of returns in respect of annual payments and distributions made by the company, together with either the payment of income tax or corporation tax due.

Late submission of a company's accounts or returns to Companies House, as well as the omission of any income or gain or excessive claims or relief, can lead to a penalty and default interest. Company books and records ought therefore to be made available to the auditors within three months of the end of the company's accounting period to enable accounts to be prepared in good time.

VAT

The directors are responsible for maintaining proper records for VAT purposes and for preparing and submitting returns to Customs and Excise. The late submission of a VAT return as well as submission of an incorrect return can give right for a penalty and default surcharge.

Approval of auditors

Article 9 LACO requires prior approval from the Audit Commission for any auditor who is appointed to audit the accounts of a regulated company. Enquiries in this respect should be addressed to the Purchasing Directorate, Audit Commission, 1 Vincent Square, London SW1P 2PN; Tel: 0171-828 1212; Fax: 0171-396 1369.

Before giving its approval to any appointment, the Commission has to be satisfied that the chosen firm has the necessary capacity and experience to undertake the audit. To enable the commission to carry out such an assessment, the following information must be provided about the chosen firm of auditors:
a) the general size and scale of operation of the firm
b) any work which the firm undertakes from the public sector
c) any other work undertaken for bus or coach operators
d) the audit date envisaged for the audit
e) the audit approach to be adopted
f) the main audit personnel, their qualifications and who will conduct the audit work.

The relevant firm must also provide a written assurance to the commission that:
i) it is an eligible auditor as described in section 389 CA
ii) it is aware of the statutory financial proprietary and financial controls governing local authority regulated companies as contained in Part V LGHA and LACO
iii) as required by LACO Article 6, that the firm is prepared to cooperate with and provide any information required by the council's own district auditors.

Specimen First Board Meeting of Company

First Meeting of the Directors of the Company

SUMMERGREEN LEISURE LIMITED

Minutes of the First Meeting of the Directors held at 36 High Road, Summergreen, SM30 2AH

Present:
Councillor Margaret Smith (in the Chair)
[names of other directors present]

1. The Chair announced that a quorum was present and declared the meeting open.

2. There was produced to the meeting the following:

2.1 The Certificate of Incorporation (under no. 0070071) dated Friday, 15 September 1995.

2.2 A print of the memorandum and articles of association of the company as registered.

2.3 A copy of form 10, the statement required under Section 2 Companies Act 1985, signed by the subscribers to the Memorandum of Association containing:

i) particulars of the first directors of the company and the first secretary of the company and their respective consents to act in the relevant capacity

ii) particulars of the intended situation of the registered office of the company.

3. It was resolved that:

3.1 Allseasons Borough Council having subscribed the memorandum and articles of association for 30,000 ordinary shares of £1 each, 30,000 such shares be allotted and issued to it in respect of such shares.

3.2 Councillor Margaret Smith be and she is hereby appointed Chair of the Directors.

3.3 The register of directors interests in shares or debentures of the company be kept at the registered office of the company.

3.4 A bank account for the company be opened with Girobank in accordance with the mandate lodged with the bank.

3.5 Messrs Brown and Smith of 2 High Street, Summergreen, Chartered Accountants (having been approved by the Audit Commission) be appointed auditors of the company and their remuneration shall be fixed by the Board.

3.6 The first accounting reference period of the company shall be changed so as to be from 15 September 1995 to 31 December 1996 and consequentially 31 December shall be the date on which in each successive calendar year an accounting period is to be treated as coming to an end.

3.7 The Secretary be instructed to arrange the filing with the Registrar of Companies of all necessary returns, including:

i) Form G88 (2) (return of allotments)

ii) Form G224 (Notice of accounting reference date).

3.8 [other resolutions which need to be passed to enable the new company to perform its functions, eg. leases, employment contracts, service level agreements, purchase of equipment, etc.]

There being no further business the meeting was terminated.

Specimen Memorandum of Council Controlled Company

Memorandum and Articles of Association of a Council Controlled Company within Part V Local Government and Housing Act 1989 in which the local authority is the sole shareholder

MEMORANDUM OF ASSOCIATION

1. The company's name is Summergreen Leisure Limited.

2. The company's registered office is situated in England.

3. The company's objects are to develop and manage the Summergreen Leisure Complex at Summergreen Road, Allseasons and the doing of all such other things as are incidental or conducive to the attainment of those objects.

4. The liability of the members is limited.

5. The company share capital is £30,000 divided into 30,000 shares of £1 each.

We the subscribers to this Memorandum of Association wish to be formed into a company pursuant to this memorandum and we agree to take the number of shares shown opposite our respective names.

Names and addresses of subscribers	Number of share taken by each
Allseasons Borough Council, Town Hall, Allseasons AS50 2HY	30,000

Signed: ....

Specimen Articles of Association of a Council Controlled Company

Private Company Limited by Shares

ARTICLES OF ASSOCIATION OF SUMMERGREEN LEISURE LIMITED

1.1   a) The regulations contained in Table A in the Companies (Tables A - F) Regulations 1985 (as amended) ('Table A') shall apply to the company except in so far as they are hereby modified or excluded. The regulations applicable to the company under any former enactment shall not apply.

b) Regulations 8 and 73 to 80 inclusive of Table A shall not apply to the company.

c) References in Table A and in these articles shall include typewriting, printing, lithography, photography, telex, fax messages, electronic mail and other means of representing or reproducing in a legible and non-transitory form.

1.2   The company is a private company and accordingly no offer shall be made to the public (whether for cash or otherwise) of any shares or debentures of the company and no allotment or agreement to allot (whether for cash or otherwise) shall be made of any shares or any debentures of the company with a view to all or any of those shares or debentures being offered for sale to the public.

2. Shares and allotment

At the date of the adoption of these articles the share capital of the company is £30,000 divided into 30,000 shares of £1 each.

3. Proceedings at general meetings

3.1   Regulation 40 of Table A shall be deleted and the following substituted therefore:

"No business shall be transacted unless a quorum is present. Three persons entitled to vote being members or duly authorised representatives of a corporation shall be a quorum".

3.2 A poll may be demanded at a general meeting by the Chair or any any member present in person and entitled to vote. Regulation 46 of Table A shall be modified accordingly.

4. Appointment, disqualification and removal of directors

4.1 A director shall not be required to hold any share qualification.

4.2 The company may by ordinary resolution appoint a person who is willing to act to be a director either to fill a vacancy or as an additional director.

4.3 Whenever and so long as the company shall be a subsidiary of another company or public body (in this article referred to as the Holding Corporation) the following provisions shall apply and to the extent of any inconsistency shall have an over-riding effect as and against all other provisions of these articles:

4.3.1 The Holding Corporation may at any time and from time to time appoint any person to be a director or remove from office any director however appointed.

4.3.2 No unissued shares shall be issued or agreed to be issued or put under any option without the consent of the Holding Corporation.

4.3.3 Any or all powers of the directors shall be restricted in such respects and to such extent as the Holding Corporation may by notice to the company from time to time lawfully prescribe.

4.3.4 So long as the Holding Corporation is the local authority or other public body the following additional restrictions shall apply:

i) A person may only be appointed or remain as a director so long as he or she is also an elected member or officer of the Holding Corporation.

ii) Only directors who are also current elected members of the Holding Corporation shall be entitled to vote at directors' meetings. Officers/directors may speak and make recommendations at directors' meetings but they cannot vote.

iii) Directors shall not receive any allowances or remuneration in respect of their office other than that arising from their membership of or employment by the Holding Corporation.

iv) So far as the company may from time to time be made subject to the provisions of Part V Local Government and Housing Act 1989 and the Local Authorities (Companies) Order 1995 (or any amendment or re-enactment thereof) the directors shall ensure that the company complies with the same at all times and neither the company nor the directors shall do (or purport to do) anything which could lead the Holding Company to act in a capacity which is *ultra vires*.

4.4 Any appointment, removal, consent or notice shall be in writing served on the company and signed on behalf of the Holding Company by an authorised signatory.

So far as the law allows, no person dealing with the company shall be concerned to see or enquire as to whether the powers of the directors have been in any way restricted hereunder, or as to whether any requisite consent of the company has been obtained and no obligation incurred or security given or transaction hereby effected by the company to or with any third party shall be invalid or ineffectual unless the third party had at that time express notice that the incurring of such obligation or the giving of such security or the effecting of such transaction was in excess of the powers of the directors.

5. Proceedings of the directors

Any director or member of a committee of directors may participate in a meeting of the directors or such committee by means of a conference, telephone or similar communications equipment whereby all participating in the meeting can hear each other and participation in such meeting in this manner shall be deemed to constitute presence at such meeting.

Names and addresses of subscribers

Allseasons Borough Council
Town Hall
Allseasons AS50 2HY

Specimen Memorandum of a Single Regeneration Budget Partnership Company

The Companies Acts 1985-1989
Company limited by Guarantee and not having a Share Capital

MEMORANDUM OF ASSOCIATION OF SPRINGWATERS
PARTNERSHIP LIMITED

1. The Company's name is 'Springwaters Partnership Limited'.

2. The Company's registered office is to be situated within England and Wales.

3. The Company's objects are to develop, foster and advance the development of that part of the Borough of Allseasons known as Springwaters ('the Area') for residential, commercial, industrial, retail, educational or social purposes; to promote and advance the improvement of the Area's cultural and environmental character and facilities; to improve transport facilities and housing; to provide assistance (whether financial or otherwise) for any of the above purposes, and such other things as are incidental or conducive to the attainment of those objects. But subject to the limitations set out in clause 4 below.

4. The powers of the company are limited as follows:
   i) The company will not engage in any speculative activities such as the trading of financial instruments.
   ii) Monies belonging to the company which are not immediately required for the objectives will be deposited only with a bank or building society authorised to accept deposits within the European Union.
   iii) The borrowing powers of the company shall (other than in exceptional circumstances) be limited to that authorised in a business plan agreed between the company and any government department which is related to the objectives set out in clause 3 above.
   iv) The company is not authorised to do anything which might put any participating local authority or other public body or any of its members or officers into a situation which is *ultra vires* or which contravenes Part V Local Government and Housing Act 1989 or the Local Authorities Companies Order 1995 or any modification or re-enactment of either (but only so far as the same is from time to time applicable to the company).

5. The income and property of the company however derived shall be applied solely towards the promotion of the objects of the company as set out in this memorandum of association and no member shall have any personal claim on any of the property of the company and no portion thereof shall be paid or transferred directly or indirectly by way of dividend, bonus or otherwise by way of profit to members of the company provided always that nothing herein shall prevent the payment in good faith by the company of a proper and reasonable remuneration to any officer or employee of the company, or to any member of the company in return for any services actually rendered to the company or interest on money lent or reasonable and proper rent for premises demised or let by any member to the company.

6. The liability of the members is limited.

7. Every member of the company undertakes to contribute such amount as may be required (not exceeding £1) to the company's assets if it should be wound up while they are a member or within one year after they cease to be a member, for payment of the company's debts and liabilities contracted before they cease to be a member, and of the costs, charges and expenses of winding up, and for the adjustment of the rights of the contributories amongst themselves.

8. If upon the winding up or dissolution of the company there remains after satisfaction of all its debts and liabilities, any property whatsoever, the same shall not be distributed amongst the members of the company, but shall be given or transferred to the local authority or local authorities with responsibility for administering public services in the Borough of Allseasons and/or to any other company or institution or other body or persons having objects similar to the objects of the company and which shall prohibit the distribution of its or their income and property amongst its or their members to an extent at least as great as imposed on the company under or by virtue of clause 5 above, and members of the company at or before the time of dissolution or in default thereof by such judge of the High Court of Justice as may have or acquired jurisdiction in the matter and if and so far as effect cannot be given to the aforesaid provisions then to another body the objects of which are charitable.

We the subscribers to this memorandum of association wish to be formed into a company pursuant to this memorandum.
Names and addresses of subscribers: ....

....

Dated: .... *1996* ....
Witness to the signatures: ....

Specimen Articles of Association of an SRB Partnership Company

The Companies Act 1985
Company limited by Guarantee and not having a Share Capital

ARTICLES OF ASSOCIATION OF SPRINGWATERS PARTNERSHIP
LIMITED

Preliminary

1. Regulations 2-35 inclusive, 54,55,57,59,102-108 inclusive, 110,114,116 and 117 of Table A shall not apply to the company but the articles hereinafter contained and, subject to the modification hereinafter expressed, the remaining regulations of Table A shall constitute the articles of association of the company.

Interpretation

2.1 In regulation 1 of Table A the definition of 'the Holder' shall be omitted.

2.2 In these articles:

'Core Members' means only the following local authorities and organisations: [list names of core members]

'Core Directors' means directors nominated to the Board of Directors by the Core Members.

'Business Members' means a chamber of commerce, business or trade organisation and companies, partnerships and sole traders engaged in trade or business and having a place of business within the Borough of Allseasons.

'Community Member' means voluntary organisations engaged in community activities within the Springwaters area of the Borough of Allseasons.

Members

3. The subscribers to the Memorandum of Association of the Company and such other persons as are admitted into membership in accordance with these articles shall be members of the company. No person shall be admitted as a member of the company unless approved by all Core Members of the company. Every person who wishes to become a member shall deliver to the company an application for membership in such form as the Core Directors require to be executed.

4.   A member may at any time withdraw from the company by giving at least seven clear days notice to the company. Membership shall not be transferable.

5.   In Regulation 38 of Table A:
a) in paragraph (b) the words "of the total voting rights at the meeting of all the members" shall be substituted for, "in nominal value of the shares giving that right" and
b) the words "the notice shall be given to all the members and to the directors and auditors" shall be substituted for the last sentence.

Proceedings at general meetings

6.   The words "and at any separate meeting of the holders of any class of shares in the company" shall be omitted from Regulation 44 of Table A.

7.   Paragraph (d) of regulation 46 of Table A shall be omitted.

8.   No business shall be transacted at any meeting unless a quorum is present. [6] persons entitled to vote on the business to be transacted, each person being a member or a proxy to a member or a duly authorised representative of a corporation shall be a quorum. [3] of such persons (or their proxies or duly authorised representatives) shall be Core Members.

Votes of members

9.   On a show of hands every member present in person shall have one vote. On a poll every member present in person or by proxy shall have one vote.

Appointment and retirement of directors

10. There shall be no maximum number of directors and the minimum number of directors shall be [8].

11. The Board will appoint as directors of the company up to [2] persons nominated by notice in writing left at the registered office of the company by each of [Allseasons Borough Council] and [Sunshire County Council] who will (in like manner) be entitled to remove either or both directors nominated by each of them and to nominate another or others in place of any director so removed or who otherwise ceases to be a director.

12. The Board will appoint as a director of the company [1] person (nominated in writing as aforesaid) by each of the other Core Members who will (in like manner) be entitled to remove a director nominated by it and to nominate another such director in the case of any other director being removed or otherwise ceasing to be a director.

13. The Board will appoint as a director of the company [1] person (approved by the Board) and nominated (by notice in writing as aforesaid) by each of the Business Members who will (in like manner) be entitled to remove a director nominated by it and to nominate another such director in place of any director so removed or otherwise ceasing to be a director.

14. The Board will appoint as a director of the company [1] person nominated (by notice in writing as aforesaid) by each of the Community Members who will (in like manner) be entitled to remove a director nominated by it and to nominate another such director in place of any director so removed or otherwise ceasing to be a director.

Borrowing powers
15. Where any plan has been agreed, from time to time with any government department with respect to the company's activities, the directors may exercise all the powers of the company to borrow money but only to the extent that the same conforms with the limits or other criteria specified in the plan.

Proceedings of directors
16. In paragraph (c) of regulation 94 of Table A the word 'debentures' shall be substituted for the words 'shares, debentures or other securities' in both places where they occur.

17. A director shall not do or omit to do anything (or suffer anything to be done or omitted to be done) which may contravene Part V Local Government and Housing Act 1989 or the Local Authorities (Companies) Order 1995 (but only so far as the same may from time to time be applicable to the company).

18. The quorum for the transaction of the business of the directors will not be less than [6] of whom [3] will be Core Directors.

Minutes
19. The words "of the holders of any class of shares in the company" shall be omitted from regulation 100 of Table A.

20. The second sentence of regulation 112 of Table A shall be omitted.

21. The words "or of the holders of any class of shares" shall be omitted from Regulation 113 of Table A.

Names and addresses of subscribers etc

Specimen Memorandum of Local Government Association

Memorandum of association for an organisation representing local authority interests which is exempted from using the word 'limited' in its name.

Memorandum of Association

Companies Acts 1985-1989

COMPANY LIMITED BY GUARANTEE AND NOT HAVING A SHARE CAPITAL

Name
1. The name of the association is 'Society of Local Authority Regulated Companies'.

Registered office
2. The registered office of the company will be situated in England.

Principal objects
3. The objects for which the association is established are:

3.1 To represent and promote the joint interests of local authority controlled or influenced companies which are regulated under the Local Authorities (Companies) Order 1995 and related legislation in the UK.

3.2 To act as a forum for ideas and advice for all local authority regulated companies and their officers.

3.3 To publish or participate in the publication of any journal or other literature or promote or participate in any exhibition, lecture or seminar which is consistent with its objects whether alone or as part of a joint arrangement with a commercial publisher or other promotional organisation.

Additional objects

4. In furtherance of the principal objects but not otherwise the association may:

4.1 Purchase, take on lease or in exchange, hire or otherwise acquire any real or personal estate which may appear convenient.

4.2 Accept any gift of property whether subject to any special trust or not, for any purpose within its principal objects.

4.3 Print or publish any periodical, leaflet or other publication.

4.4 Sell, lease, mortgage or otherwise deal with all or any part of the property of the society.

4.5 Borrow and raise money to secure its repayment.

4.6 Invest the funds of the society in or upon such investments, securities or property as may be thought fit.

4.7 Subscribe to any local or other charities or benevolent objects, and grant donations for any public, general or useful purpose.

4.8 Purchase or otherwise acquire and undertake all or any part of the property, assets, liabilities and engagements of any body with which the society is authorised to amalgamate.

4.9 Transfer all or any part of the property, assets, liabilities and engagements of the society to any body with which the society is authorised to amalgamate.

4.10 Do all other lawful things as are incidental or conducive to the attainment of any of the principal objects.

Application of income and property
5. The entire income and property of the society must be applied solely towards the promotion of the objects of the society as set out in this memorandum; and no distribution may be paid or transferred directly or indirectly by way of dividend or bonus or otherwise by way of profit to the persons who at any time are or have been members of the society or to any of them, or to any person claiming through any of them providing that nothing contained in this Memorandum of Association prevents:

5.1 Payment in good faith of remuneration to any member of the society or other person in return for any services actually rendered to the society.

5.2 Payment of interest at a reasonable rate (to be determined by the Management Committee) on money borrowed from a member of the society.

5.3   Free distribution among, or sale at a discount to, members of the society of any books, forms or other publications (whether published or issued by the society or otherwise) or free or concessionary attendance to any exhibition, lecture or seminar as aforesaid.

Liability

6.   The liability of the members is limited.

Contributions

7.   Every member of the society undertakes to contribute to the assets of the society in the event of its being wound up while it is a member or within one year afterwards for payment of the debts and liabilities of the society contracted before it ceases to be a member and for the cost, charges and expenses of winding up, and for the adjustment of the rights of the contributories amongst themselves, such amount as may be required not exceeding £1.

Winding up

8.   If on the winding up or dissolution of the society, any property remains after satisfaction of all debts and liabilities, that property must not be paid to or distributed among members of the society but must be given or transferred to some other institution having objects similar to the society to be determined by the members of the society, and in default by any judge of the High Court of Justice who may have acquired jurisdiction in this matter, and if and so far as effect cannot be given to this provision, then to some other charitable object.

Names and addresses of subscribers etc

Specimen Articles for Local Government Association

Articles of Association for organisation representing local authority interests and exempted from using word 'limited'

– Articles of Association
– Companies Act 1985-1989
– Company Limited by Guarantee and not having a Share Capital

ARTICLES OF ASSOCIATION OF SOCIETY OF LOCAL AUTHORITY REGULATED COMPANIES

1. Interpretation
1.1 'The Act' means the Companies Act 1985 including any statutory modification or re-enactment of it from time to time in force:

1.1.2 'Clear days' in relation to the period of notice means that period excluding the day the notice is given and the day for which it is to take effect.

1.1.3 'Management Committee' means the management committee of the society.

1.1.4 'The Society' means the Society of Local Authority Regulated Companies.

1.2 Unless the context otherwise requires, words or expressions contained in these articles bear the same meaning as in the Act but excluding any statutory modification of it not in force when these articles became binding on the society.

2. Objects
The Society is established for the purposes expressed in the Memorandum of Association.

3. Membership
3.1 The persons who are members of the society at the date of the adoption of these articles and such local authorities and other public sector organisations as are elected members in accordance with the regulations for the time being of the society and no other persons may be members of the society.
4. Officers

4.1 There must be a Chair, a Vice Chair, a Treasurer and a Secretary ('the officers') who must be elected by the society at the annual general meeting and hold office until the day after the next annual general meeting but who may be re-elected.

4.2 There must be a Management Committee consisting of:

i) The Chair, Vice Chair, Treasurer and Secretary for the time being.

ii) [7] other persons elected at the annual general meeting for one year or until the day after the next annual general meeting but who may be re-elected for successive years.

iii) If a casual vacancy occurs in any of the offices or among the elected members of the Management Committee between one annual general meeting and the next, the Management Committee may appoint a member to fill the vacancy; but the member so appointed may hold office only until the day after the next annual general meeting unless at such meeting they are elected for a further period.

iv) The Management Committee may continue to act even though the total number of its members is reduced by death, retirement or otherwise below the number of [7] (plus Chair, Vice Chair, Treasurer and Secretary) but if at any time the number is reduced below [4] the continuing members of the Management Committee shall act only to fill vacancies until there are at least [7] members of the Management Committee together with a Chair, Vice Chair, Treasurer and Secretary.

5. Annual General Meeting

5.1 The Society must hold an annual general meeting each year in addition to any other meetings in that year and must specify the meeting as such in the notices calling it.

5.2 Not more than 15 months may elapse between one annual general meeting of the society and the next.

5.3 The annual general meeting must be held on such date and time as the Management Committee appoints.

5.4 At the annual general meeting the report of the Management Committee and the accounts for the previous year must be considered, calls upon the members may be made, officers and other elected members of the Management Committee for the following years must be elected (by ballot if the number of nominations exceeds the number of vacancies), and any other business may be transacted that may be transacted at an annual general meeting by statute or by these articles.

5.5 All general meetings other than the annual general meeting must be called extraordinary general meetings.

6. Convening Annual General Meetings

6.1 The Management Committee may, whenever it thinks fit, and must upon a requisition made in writing by [10] or more members convene an extraordinary general meeting.

6.2 Any requisition for an extraordinary general meeting must express the object of the meeting proposed to be called and must be left or sent by recorded delivery post to the registered office of the society and addressed to the secretary.

6.3 On receipt of such requisition the Management Committee must proceed to convene an extraordinary general meeting.

6.4 If the Committee does not proceed to convene the meeting within 21 days from receiving the requisition the relevant members or any 10 members may themselves convene such a meeting.

7. Notice of meetings

7.1 At least 21 clear days notice of every annual general meeting and 14 days notice of every other general meeting must be given.

7.2 The notice must specify the place, day and time of the meeting and in the case of special business the general nature of such business must be sent by ordinary pre-paid post to each member.

8. Business

All business is deemed to be special with the exception of business that may be transacted at the annual general meeting according to these articles.

9. Copy of minutes to be sent to members

A copy of the proceedings of an annual general meeting must be sent to each member.

10. Voting

10.1 At every general meeting [10] members form a quorum.

10.2 Each member may have one vote and except in cases otherwise specifically provided for in these articles all questions must be decided by a majority of the members present and voting and the Chair, in case of equality, may have a second or casting vote.

10.3 Any question which the Management Committee (or any [10] or more members) considers to be of major general importance shall be put to a postal ballot of the entire membership. A decision shall then be made on the basis of a majority of the votes returned.

11. Exercise of powers of management committee

11.1 The management of the society must be entrusted to the Management Committee which may:

i) Regulate its own meetings.

ii) Fix the quorum necessary for the transaction of business at its meetings.

iii) Delegate any of its powers to special committees or sub-committees consisting of members of the Management Committee or of other members of the society.

iv) Make, alter and revoke bylaws or regulations so long as any bylaws and regulations are not inconsistent to these articles.

v) Generally exercise all powers of the society that are not by these articles or by statute required to be exercised by the society in general meetings.

11.2 No resolution by the society in general meeting may invalidate any prior act of the Management Committee which would have been valid had a resolution not been made.

11.3 The Management Committee must make a report to every general meeting.

12. Application for membership

12.1 Every organisation which wishes to be admitted as a member of the society must complete and forward a written application for membership to the secretary.

12.2 Every application for membership must be submitted to the Management Committee at the next available meeting or at a subsequent meeting as soon as it is practicable to do so.

13. Approval of membership application

An application for membership of the society must be approved by a majority of the members of the Management Committee present and voting.

14. Entrance fee

Every new member elected under these articles must upon its submission to the society pay such entrance fee (if any) as is fixed by the bylaws in force and any subscription or any portion of a subscription that has been made under article 19.

15. Expulsion of members

If any member is accused of any improper act or omission which the Management Committee after investigation considers to be seriously prejudicial to the interests of the society or its objects, an extraordinary general meeting of the society must be convened to consider the accusation (of which the accused must have had [14] clear days notice). The accused may, after it has had the opportunity of explaining its conduct, by a vote of three-quarters of the members present and voting on the question, be expelled from the society and will then forfeit their interest and privileges in the society without further claim for subscriptions or any other money paid to the society, but they will remain liable to pay any subscriptions or other money outstanding at the date of expulsion.

16. Rights of membership

The rights of each member are personal and not capable of assignment.

17. Resignation of membership

Any member having paid all money due to the society may resign their membership on giving one month's notice in writing to the secretary of their intention to do so.

18. Accounts

18.1 (Subject to any statutory exemptions or concessions) auditors shall be appointed and their duties regulated in accordance with the Companies Act 1985.

18.2 A copy of every balance sheet (including every document required by law to be annexed to the balance sheet) which is to be laid before the society in general meeting together (if applicable) with a copy of the auditors report must, not less than 21 days before the date of the meeting, be sent to every member of the society.

19. Funds

The Management Committee may from time to time determine the amount of subscriptions to be charged to members and each member must pay such subscription to the treasurer at such time or times as the same falls due.

20. Forfeiture of membership

Any member who has not paid their subscription by the end of the current year to which it relates may be struck off the roll of members by resolution of the Management Committee.

21. Notices

21.1 Any notice to be served by the society upon any member may be served either personally or by sending it through the post in a pre-paid letter addressed to their nominated representative.

21.2 Any notice if served by post is presumed to have been served at the time the letter containing the notice would be delivered in the ordinary course of post, and a certificate signed by the secretary or the person employed by them to post the notice is conclusive evidence for the notice having been duly posted.

22. Members' addresses

Every member must from time to time notify the secretary of their address.

23. Headings

The headings in these articles are not part of the articles and do not affect the interpretation or construction of the articles in any way.

Names and addresses of subscribers etc

Appendix H

OYEZ

Please complete in
typescript, or in
bold black capitals.

Notes on completion appear on final page.

First Directors and Secretary and Intended Situation of Registered Office

F0100C10

Company Name in full SUMMERGREEN LEISURE LIMITED

Proposed Registered Office (PO Box numbers only, are not acceptable) 36 HIGH ROAD

Post town SUMMERGREEN

County/Region SUNSHIRE   Postcode AS50 0BX

If the memorandum is delivered by an agent for the subscriber(s) of the memorandum mark the box opposite and give the agent's name and address.

Agent's Name MICHAEL SMITH

Address TOWN HALL

Post town SUMMERGREEN

County/Region SUNSHIRE   Postcode AS50 0BX

Number of continuation sheets attached. 3

Please give the name, address, telephone number, and if available, a DX number and Exchange of the person Companies House should contact if there is any query.

MICHAEL SMITH
TOWN HALL, ALLSEASONS
Tel 01634 - 810810

DX number   DX exchange

When you have completed and signed the form please send it to the Registrar of Companies at:
Companies House, Crown Way, Cardiff, CF4 3UZ
for companies registered in England and Wales   **DX 33050 Cardiff**
or
Companies House, 37 Castle Terrace, Edinburgh, EH1 2EB
for companies registered in Scotland   **DX 235 Edinburgh**
[P.T.O.

87

Company Secretary (see notes 1-5)

Company Name: SUMMERGREEN LEISURE LIMITED

*Voluntary details. **NAME**

*Style/Title: MR
*Honours etc.:

Forename(s): JOHN

Surname: JONES

Previous forename(s):

Previous surname(s):

Address: 22 SUNSHIRE ROAD

Usual residential address
For a corporation, give the registered or principal office address.

Post town: SUMMERGREEN

County/Region: SUNSHIRE   Postcode: AS50 4B+

Country: ENGLAND

I consent to act as secretary of the company named on page 1

Consent signature: J-Jones   Date: 6/9/95

Directors (see notes 1-5)
Please list directors in alphabetical order.

NAME

*Style/Title: COUNCILLOR   *Honours etc.:

Forename(s): MARGARET

Surname: SMITH

Previous forename(s):

Previous surname(s):

Address: 63 APRICOT TERRACE

Usual residential address
For a corporation, give the registered or principal office address.

Post town: ALLSEASONS

County/Region: SUNSHIRE   Postcode: AS50 8PA

Country: ENGLAND

Day	Month	Year
12	4	45

Date of birth   Nationality: BRITISH

Business occupation: HOUSEWIFE

Other directorships:

I consent to act as director of the company named on page 1

Consent signature: Margaret Smith   Date: 6/9/95

88

Directors (continued) (see notes 1–5)

NAME	*Style/Title	COUNCILLOR	*Honours etc.	

*Voluntary details.

Forename(s): STEPHEN VIVIAN

Surname: DOBSON

Previous forename(s):

Previous surname(s):

Address: 38 PERCY ROAD

Usual residential address
For a corporation, give the
registered or principal office
address.

Post town: SUMMERGREEN

County/Region: SUNSHIRE   Postcode: AS50 8NT

Country: ENGLAND

Day	Month	Year
8	11	50

Date of birth: 8 11 50   Nationality: BRITISH

Business occupation: ENGINEER

Other directorships:

I consent to act as director of the company named on page 1

Consent signature: S. Dobson   Date: 4/9/95

This section must be signed by

Either
an agent on behalf
of all subscribers

Signed: M. Smith   Date: 8/9/95

Or the subscribers
(i.e. those who signed
as members on the
memorandum of
association).

Signed: Date:

Signed: Date:

Signed: Date:

Signed: Date:

Signed: Date:

Signed: Date:

Appendix I

12

Declaration on Application for Registration

OYEZ
Please complete in typescript, or in bold black capitals.

F0120C10

Company Name in full SUMMERGREEN LEISURE LIMITED

I, MICHAEL SMITH

of TOWN HALL, ALLSEASONS, ASS 2HY

do solemnly and sincerely declare that I am a [Solicitor engaged in the formation of the company] [person named as director or secretary of the company in the statement delivered to the Registrar under section 10 of the Companies Act 1985]† and that all the requirements of the Companies Act 1985 in respect of the registration of the above company and of matters precedent and incidental to it have been complied with.

And I make this solemn Declaration conscientiously believing the same to be true and by virtue of the Statutory Declarations Act 1835.

†Please delete as appropriate.

Declarant's signature M Smith

Declared at SUMMERGREEN

the 9th day of September

One thousand nine hundred and ninety Five

Please print name.

before me* GRAHAM LAW

Signed G - Law Date 9/9/95

A Commissioner for Oaths or Notary Public or Justice of the Peace or Solicitor

Please give the name, address, telephone number, and if available, a DX number and Exchange of the person Companies House should contact if there is any query.

MICHAEL SMITH, TOWN HALL ALLSEASONS ASSO 2HY Tel 01636 - 810810

DX number   DX exchange

When you have completed and signed the form please send it to the Registrar of Companies at:
Companies House, Crown Way, Cardiff, CF4 3UZ
for companies registered in England and Wales   **DX 33050 Cardiff**
or
Companies House, 37 Castle Terrace, Edinburgh, EH1 2EB
for companies registered in Scotland   **DX 235 Edinburgh**

OYEZ The Solicitors' Law Stationery Society Ltd, Oyez House, 7 Spa Road, London SE16 3QQ

Companies 12

1995 Edition
2.95 F29025
5017173
★ ★ ★ ★ ★

Index

91